"Too often, the ugliness of sin and the brokenness of our world cause us to lose sight of the beauty of our God. *Searching for Spring* reminds us of this beauty, of the wonders of God's creation and Christ's promise to make all things new. Read and wonder as Christine Hoover teaches us to see the beauty and hope ever-present amid the pain."

Russell Moore, president, The Ethics
and Religious Liberty Commission

"Of all the things that can scuttle our faith, forgetting the goodness and beauty of God must top the list. In *Searching for Spring*, Hoover calls us to encounter a God whose heart beats with goodness and beauty—a God who persists and *insists* on 'making all things beautiful in their time.' This is a book that you will want to read slowly, allowing its hope-filled message to saturate the corners of your weary, doubting soul."

Hannah Anderson, author of *Humble Roots: How
Humility Grounds and Nourishes Your Soul*

"Christine Hoover's book *Searching for Spring* opened my eyes to the wonder and beauty God creates during difficult seasons. If you are looking for an encouraging, hope-filled book, then this one is for you. Christine, by highlighting biblical truth, helps bring life to the very places within that feel dead."

Kelly Balarie, author, speaker, and blogger
at www.purposefulfaith.com

"In times of trial or the bleakest of days, we do find hope, like Job, knowing that no purpose of God's 'can be thwarted' (Job 42:2). However, often we still struggle when we can't see exactly how God is working. Christine Hoover's *Searching for Spring* provides a wonderful reflection on how to live

in a bleak world, hoping in God and yet still struggling. I commend it highly, as this kind of message is one we cannot hear enough. May this book rise above and drown out the many other voices of despair in our world and in our minds."

Jason G. Duesing, provost and associate professor
of historical theology, Midwestern Baptist
Theological Seminary, Kansas City, Missouri

"Like Narnian creatures, we're tempted in the isolating, bitter cold moments of the Christian life to feel as if it's 'always winter and never Christmas.' In *Searching for Spring*, Christine Hoover shows us that, even in winter, our God is working in our lives. This is a book that invites the reader to slow down, look around, and rejoice in the hope of the coming warmth of spring."

Catherine Parks, author of *A Christ-Centered Wedding*;
blogger at cathparks.com

"Christine has a unique ability to weave words of biblical truths, compelling real-life stories, and practical application into a gorgeous tapestry. This gift is beautifully evident in her newest book, *Searching for Spring*. Whether you find yourself in a season of bitter emptiness, pain-filled brokenness, or unexpected suffering, Christine will point your heart to the beauty that can be hoped for in every situation."

Katie Orr, creator of the FOCUSed15 Bible studies

"'In his time . . .' daunting words for the soul waiting for redemption, healing, or restoration. Yet God has a beautiful, mysterious cycle of rebirth that resembles the four seasons. Christine Hoover reminds us in our winter that spring is coming. For those dangling in hopelessness, this book is for you."

Kathy Litton, Send Network leader and pastor's wife

SEARCHING FOR SPRING

HOW GOD MAKES ALL THINGS
BEAUTIFUL IN TIME

CHRISTINE HOOVER

BakerBooks
a division of Baker Publishing Group
Grand Rapids, Michigan

Published by Baker Books
a division of Baker Publishing Group
PO Box 6287, Grand Rapids, MI 49516-6287
www.bakerbooks.com

Printed in the United States of America

Library of Congress Cataloging-in-Publication Data
Names: Hoover, Christine, author.
Title: Searching for spring : how God makes all things beautiful in time / Christine Hoover.
Description: Grand Rapids : Baker Books, 2018. | Includes bibliographical references.
Identifiers: LCCN 2017043746 | ISBN 9780801019388 (pbk.)
Subjects: LCSH: Christian women—Religious life. | Aesthetics—Religious aspects—Christianity. | Spirituality—Christianity. | Spiritual life—Christianity.
Classification: LCC BV4527 .H6637 2018 | DDC 248.8/43—dc23
LC record available at https://lccn.loc.gov/2017043746

The author is represented by the literary agency of Wolgemuth & Associates, Inc.

18 19 20 21 22 23 24   7 6 5 4 3 2 1

In keeping with biblical principles of creation stewardship, Baker Publishing Group advocates the responsible use of our natural resources. As a member of the Green Press Initiative, our company uses recycled paper when possible. The text paper of this book is composed in part of post-consumer waste.

For my parents, who have given me so much,
and for Amy, Marylyn, and Susan,
cherished friends who are waiting
and watching for all things
to be made beautiful

CONTENTS

Contents

The day the Lord created hope was probably the same day He created spring.

Bernard Williams

PART ONE

SUMMER

He has made everything beautiful in its time.

Ecclesiastes 3:11

Hide and Seek

For everything there is a season, and a time for
every matter under heaven.

MOM, IS LIFE HARD?"
My oldest son, sitting beside me in the car, sliced
the silence with this profound question. I glanced over at
him, my mind jarred from running through my errand list,
attempting to discern his motivation for asking, trying not
to panic. *Has something bad happened to him? Does he
see something in me that is inadvertently teaching him life
is joyless? Has he overheard someone's litany of suffering?
To what underlying despair in him have I been oblivious?*

My son, however, gave no indication of anything other
than curiosity. His green eyes settled on me, waiting for a
response.

"Why do you ask?" I prompted, looking for a target that might help me formulate an answer.

"I just wondered. You told me you like having conversations in the car, so I was just starting a conversation."

Relieved and amused, I smiled. The day before, tired of prodding for even the slightest details from my three boys, I had told them how much I enjoy conversation with them, hoping they'd get the hint. Apparently at least one of them had, and now I'd been lobbed quite the philosophical question. The joke, it seemed, was on me.

How could I answer truthfully without also shattering his youthful optimism and innocence?

My instinctual internal answer was yes; life is certainly difficult in many, many ways. Bolstering my claim, I mentally ticked through the experiences of those closest to me in the past year alone: my friend who's navigated heartbreak and confusion, our family friends who've lost their wife and mother to cancer, my parents who've already cared for one set of aging parents and are currently caring for another set, and a dear one who's not so sure she can or wants to obey God because of what it's costing her. This world, it seemed to me in that moment of searching for an answer, is pockmarked with decay and broken hearts. Sometimes I feel heavy and paralyzed by it all—the injustice, oppression, and how everything doesn't turn out the way I'd like it to be.

Should I tell him that? *You don't know it fully yet, but in this world you will be hurt, betrayed, and beaten down by life. And you don't know it fully yet, but some of the pain will be from your own doing.*

And yet there is so much more. The roller coaster doesn't just plunge; it also climbs to exhilarating heights. Life gifts

14

us with the joys of belly laughter, the sight of baby chub, the taste of apple pie, the smell of ocean spray, and the touch of someone you love loving you. At certain moments, living is the easiest thing in the world to do.

I certainly wanted to tell him that, to give him eyes to see everything there is to see beyond video games and fleeting youthful desires.

But at some point, pain will find him; I cannot protect him from it, so I must find a way to tell him the truth about it. He's like a child in the middle of summer who believes the light and carefree innocence and enveloping warmth will forever remain the same. He wholeheartedly believes summer's story, and, as all parents do, I want desperately to give him this fairy tale. Even more, though, I want to be the one to tell him that we all, every single one, are vulnerable to pain. Summer always gives way to fall, sometimes in the span of one breath.

I thought about what I'd been told as a teenager when events unfolded that exposed my own vulnerability to pain: "Attitude is everything." I know what that well-intentioned person meant—that I should choose to look at what's going well, choose to think the best of that person or circumstance that was bothering me, choose a positive perspective. The person who said those words was my counselor, which may go a long way in explaining *why* he said it. I am a person prone to despair, prone to seeing what's wrong rather than what's right. Back then, I'd been drowning for lack of truth and an overabundance of irrational emotion, and attitude actually *wasn't* everything. I couldn't positive-think my way to an obstacle-free life, nor a happy one at that. My son, with his startling conversation starter, could not have known how much I'd considered the very things he was asking me about.

No, attitude is not everything. I know that now, sure enough. The wisest man who's ever lived said that God has made everything beautiful in its time.

Beauty is everything, and beauty lies at the heart of all of life for all of time, even and especially where we think it couldn't possibly exist—in the hurt, in betrayal, and when life seems to be beating you down.

Beauty is the drumbeat that began playing on the earth's birthday and has never stopped since, a bass drum pulsing beneath all we see and touch and taste and experience in this life, urging us to march on into battle.

The mallet hits in rhythm: God has made everything to be beautiful in the past.

Again: God will make everything turn out beautiful in the future.

And again: God is currently working to make all things beautiful right at this very moment.

Everything? This is difficult to believe, because few things are currently beautiful, and we, from our own experiences, know the reality of ugliness far more intimately than we know the truth of all things being beautiful.

But just because we can't see how God has made and is making all things beautiful doesn't mean it's not true. It just means we must know where to look and where to listen, because only those who listen begin to hear beauty's rhythm.

Hidden in Plain Sight

Our neighborhood, tucked at the base of a mountain, piled high with trees, holds a menagerie of animals. As I return home at dusk, my car headlights find the reflective eyes of a red fox my boys have named Finn. At summer dawn, as I make my morning coffee, I spy a doe and her fawn eating the ivy growing at the crest of the creek behind our house. Ruby-throated hummingbirds, who bid us farewell in the winter, return in summer to buzz at the feeder. Spiders draw their webs at the corner of our porch, seeking refuge in the overhang. Cardinals perch in the trees year round, making nests in our bushes and once even in our mailbox. Woodpeckers mistake our chimney for a tree, sending reverberations all through our house. Squirrels and blue jays fight for dominance in the front yard as brown rabbits dart by. Turtles, like frail old men, drag themselves through the tall summer grass.

There is one animal, however, I know is there but have yet to see.

My husband once collected our boys for show-and-tell in the lawn mower shed. Inside, he'd discovered a six-foot-long snakeskin dangling from the electrical cord on the wall. The boys, of course, pulsed with excitement and have taken all subsequent houseguests on a personalized snakeskin tour, complete with surprise touches to the guest's back and imitation hiss noises in their ear as they gingerly step down into the dimly lit shed.

I am thankful to have only seen the snakeskin and not the actual snake, but its presence made me consider what other animals might be living their whole existence around us without us even knowing. How many times have I been doing chores while a doe is giving birth in my backyard brush? How many times have I been scrolling through my phone while an eagle is soaring overhead? What insects wriggle underfoot as we play in the yard? How close are black bears sleeping to my own resting place?

How many animals have I *not* seen?

My boys and I have discussed this, delighted to imagine all the miracles happening around us. We have become seekers of all that is hidden in plain sight. When one of us sees something on the porch or through a window, we call out to the others: a walking stick! A hawk! Blooms on the dogwood tree! A goldfinch at the bird feeder! *Come and see!*

The way the world is designed gives heft to the drumbeat pulsing beneath time.

For instance, doesn't the cicada, waiting seven years underground, tell us something about beauty? Doesn't it coax us to *come and see* and then, in wonder, *go and seek* where this incredible cicada came from and what it communicates about its Creator?

We must be perpetual seekers in a cosmic game of Hide and Seek.

We think we know beauty when we see it, and we're sure we know where to seek it. Art in the gallery. Carefully written words on the page. Fit and well-clothed bodies. And especially the natural world. As a human race, we flock to beaches and mountains *en masse*, longing for escape from the manmade, longing for the wonder of things we didn't make. We can only exist between skyscrapers for so long before we must decamp to juicy strawberries, stargazer lilies, snowflakes, and turquoise water. The sounds of the ocean and falling rain calm us, so much so that we sleep to artificial re-creations of moving water. We marvel at the views from our mountaintop perch, love the sand between our toes, and even those among us who don't believe in God seek peace in the very place that shouts about him—nature.

If I miss the owl, the skunk, or the butterfly in my own front yard, it's likely I'm missing so much of the beauty and wonder

God is weaving into my life. I miss his movement because I am busy with many things and, even more so, am distracted. I reject or resist the means by which he desires to build and unveil beauty inside of me, turning away from obstacles, difficulties, and unfulfilled longings, so certain beauty is not hiding there.

In the lifelong game of Hide and Seek, is nature the final word in beauty? We certainly could spend decades sinking into the far-reaching depths of its physical glory, but of all we're instinctively drawn toward as human beings, it's perhaps the *unseen* that cues our hearts to come alive: virtuous acts done for a stranger, true words spoken, unexplained generosity, help given in a time of crisis, decades-long fidelity, forgiveness in the face of hate, sacrificial service, a chosen purity in a decadent world, determination and joy in the midst of suffering, or a hopeless case changed. Clarion moments, all, that prick us awake from our routines and our numbness, singing inexplicable sounds of joy into our bleak existence. For fleeting moments, we see what's hidden in plain sight and something inside whispers: *there is meaning to life; there is beauty unfolding.*

The intangible beauty of a transformed life sings the loudest of all, for no one can resist it and no one can refute it: the alcoholic staying sober, the gangbanger turning into a counselor to young men on the street, the racist with a humbled and changed perspective. Just as we gravitate toward the natural world, we love stories of overcoming, of wrong turned right, of justice and love, because all are signposts to something bigger, something greater, something even more beautiful at work.

And yet eyes cannot always see and ears cannot always hear.

This is, in fact, why life can be hard—because we have trouble seeing what's hidden in plain sight. Our hearts are blind; we struggle to define beauty properly or in a way that leads to wonder—to God. We define beauty in ways that are finite and, often, self-serving or self-gratifying. We are a people content with calling a purse or a cityscape beautiful, ascribing ultimate value to decaying and lifeless things. Our definition of beauty limits, confines, and destroys our own joy, because decaying or lifeless things cannot produce unending beauty nor can they transform a life.

What if beauty could actually be found in the very things our skewed hearts deem ugly? What if all that we resist—suffering, confession, brokenness, loneliness, death—were the very things in process of becoming beautiful? All of these experiences are painful, but each can produce or lead us to the unexpected beauty of perseverance, hope, redemption, heaven, and God himself.

That is precisely the point: God is beautiful. All he's created points back to him, reflecting who he is and what he's like. Forgiveness and reconciliation, justice and mercy, peace and joy—a life transformed—point back to him. He is beauty hiding in plain sight, leaving clues as to his whereabouts through both his artistic words ("And God said, 'Let there be light,' and there was light" [Gen. 1:3]) and his written words. He calls us to come and seek, so we can *come and see*, so we may discover how everything—*everything*—he touches turns beautiful in time to reflect his own beauty. That means me and my life, and you and your life, even the most hopeless and dark parts. When we dig beyond the cicada's design and the transformed life in search of God, we find a beauty that drives out despair and adds color to muted, mundane days. He in turn hands us beauty to fight hopelessness in the difficulties of life, and he offers beauty as a present medicine for our souls.

Oh, how we need this medicine!

We need it not only to battle despair but also to wake from our numb distraction. We're made to be beauty seekers but too often we're merely surviving. We are restless from a lack of wonder and sometimes we're pierced by more than just restlessness: depression, anxiety, apathy, bitterness, and hopelessness. We exist in a crafted busyness where we attempt to silence our heart's craving. What is the point of seeking beauty anyway? Why awaken our hearts to the risk of emotion when life's pain is too deep?

Because beauty is the most potent weapon we have with which to fight back.

Beauty Needs Time

But here's why we prefer numb hearts rather than alive ones: beauty is not immediate. It often unveils itself slowly, through much waiting, much seeking, and sometimes much heartache.

The cicada and the wise man tell us this as well. The wise man said, "[God] has made everything beautiful *in its time*" (Eccles. 3:11). The cicada proves this truth by waiting seven years before continuing his story, which happens to be prompt reproduction and then death. In the cosmic game of Hide and Seek, it seems there is a big picture element to beauty, one we must embrace in order to find it.

Because the most beautiful beauty—a transformed life—is not immediate, we must be patient, lifetime seekers, not only

21

mining our past and present circumstances for beauty but also cultivating a hope for future beauty.

I find it difficult to fully comprehend beauty in the present anyway, for I can only see the present through a glass dimly. In a moment where I try to etch a joyful occasion on my heart, I can't quite wrap myself completely around it. When I'm holding my husband's hand across the table on our wedding anniversary, I'm overcome with joy at being married to such a man. But then a little bit of fear creeps in. *What if he's taken away from me? What if the future holds dire and difficult things for us?* I tell myself to enjoy the moment, but pure beauty has been eclipsed by my fear. In the present moment, I cannot escape my distractible emotions.

This is why beauty needs time. We comprehend and value true beauty most significantly over time. Once again, come with me to my anniversary table as I'm holding the hands of my beloved husband. As he and I discuss the years we've had together, recalling stories of our newlywed days and the rough patches along the way to eighteen years, I see the beauty of our love so clearly in time past. I recognize how the struggles firmed our commitment to one another. I rejoice in all the Lord has helped us overcome and how he's used our partnership for his glory. There is no fear to eclipse the beauty this time, only concrete years displaying very real beauty that makes me hopeful for the future and happy in the present.

And so it is with God and why he doesn't make all things beautiful immediately. Before the unveiling of the complete transformation he's made in us, we have an opportunity that will vanish when all is made beautiful: the opportunity for faith. Our faith pleases him so, and this is not a faith built upon happy emotions. This is a faith built upon something concrete: what beauty he's already orchestrated in time and what beauty he says he will make in time beyond. We may not be able to see and comprehend clearly all of what God is doing in the present, but we can always mine the past and the future for treasures.

This is the pattern of Scripture, really. In the Old Testament, God repetitiously required his people to build altars, recall stories of his acts to their children, and celebrate feasts that marked the miracles he'd done on their behalf. Over and over, he said to them, "Remember." They were to remember how God made freedom from slavery and provision from lack so they'd trust him in their present.

Then, as the drumbeat played on, God's refrain through the prophets became, "Look forward." They were to look forward to a perfect deliverer and forever rescuer, when God would make beauty from their ashes, so that they might trust him with those ashes in their present state.

In the New Testament, the pattern of the Old Testament emerges. After the Gospels, the writers point back to the death and resurrection of Christ and then forward to his future coming, all so that we'd look at the past with gratefulness and awe, the future with faith, and the present with eyes wide open to beauty and hope.

Look back. God has created and God has come.

Look ahead. God will come again.

A question emerges, no matter where we stand in the timeline of history: And so, having looked behind and ahead, how can we live now in light of who he is?

In all of it, the pulse of the beauty of God has played in seen and unseen places, and we'll spend the rest of this book playing in a big game of Hide and Seek. We'll do this by discovering the heartbeat of God that's moved him to action on our behalf. We'll find out how he's still acting, working to bring all of time to a culmination when all things will be made right and beauty will be forever. As we look at how God has acted and is acting, we can then know what we must do and how we must live in response. This is a book that describes how faith—waiting for All Things Beautiful—is lived out in real life.

Why? So you can live alive today, you can know rest and peace, you can face whatever you're facing with hope, you can do the work you've been given. So you can obey even though obedience costs and even hurts sometimes. So you can see beauty rising and worship God.

I looked over at my precious boy, enveloped in innocence, and answered him as truthfully as I could. "Son, life is definitely hard. People in this world face challenges and difficulties beyond what you know or might imagine. But then there are great joys in life, and they seem to go together somehow. Like when I had you, it was painful and I was scared, but then you were born and you've been one of the greatest gifts in my life. That joy came out of suffering. And so it is with some of the best things in life. God takes our difficulty and flips it on its head, wringing out beauty."

It turns out the instinctual answer—yes, life is hard—is also the incomplete answer. There is a long and winding answer, an essay answer, even a saga answer that plays out over generations. There is so much more to life than difficulty; there is also beauty. And sometimes the most profound beauty is discovered in and through the difficulty. In fact, at the heart of Christianity is the hope that this is true, that God is making everything beautiful in its time.

What about you? At some point—and perhaps you are experiencing it currently—we all hold shattered dreams in our hands; we all are downtrodden, boats taking on water in a raging ocean. Hope fades and we become the boy in the car asking his mama if this is what life is like. You don't need an attitude adjustment, nor do you need pithy clichés of positive thinking. You need the truth, and here it is: God can make something beautiful out of you, even the most hopeless, broken-down thing in your life, *especially* that. The beauty will most likely come—you need to hear this, dear one—through pain, waiting, wrestling, and difficulty.

I know you mourn the passing of summer, those years of your life when you were full of innocence and high-flying dreams. I know you question whether the blossom can come after the winter you're in. I know you wonder if God is at work or if he's even there at all. I know, most of all, you want the ends without the means. I want to protect you, as I want to protect my son, from the means, to distract you from the honest-to-goodness truth that pain can be for our good, but in the end I cannot do that, because I would be protecting you from beauty itself.

This book is a story about death-defying hope. Despair-defying hope. It's also about pain—your pain, the variety of which you think of first when you wake in the night, the kind wrapping its tentacles around you right at this very moment. This story requests you take a giant step backward in an attempt to scan as much of the horizon as possible, and then it invites you to hold a magnifying glass up to your current experience, searching for the hidden treasures in your life. This is the story of the most dazzling beauty blooming under the surface of all we can see with our eyes.

Come and see how God makes everything beautiful in its time.

PART TWO

FALL

Don't you ever wonder why
In spite of all that's wrong here
There's still so much that goes so right
And beauty abounds?

Andrew Peterson

Marred Beauty

> For everything there is a season, and a time for
> every matter under heaven: *a time to be born,*
> *and a time to die.*

I'M NOT SURE I WOULD CALL MYSELF AN ARTIST, but
I love to decorate my home. Although I'm grateful when
others compliment my choices, I don't decorate to impress.
I decorate because aesthetics make me feel things, and en-
vironment is important to me. I want to use the colors and
patterns that speak to me in order to speak to others.

When my husband comes to bed after an arduous day, I
want him to slip into deep rest and enjoy with me the relationship we've cultivated together. A crisp white comforter
and fluffy pillows, to me, invite those very things. Soft lights

and warm affection communicate a place of security and acceptance.

When friends come over, I want them to sit around my table (or, as they inevitably do, stand over the chips and salsa at the kitchen counter) and feel they are safe, that they belong, that they are loved. Good food, decorative touches to the dinner table, and intentional questions are the tools I use to communicate such sentiments.

Sometimes I am the spoken to, transported by the art of others.

My friend Joseph writes music, giving voice to songs my heart longs to sing.

Young women in my church—Stephanie, Marieke, Ashley, and Holly—capture photographs of intangible things like love and family.

April paints abstract and watercolor paintings using colors that infuse joy into me.

No matter the medium, every artist attempts to order and design in such a way that their intended truth is communicated. It's why they do what they do.

Before any other artist, the Artist who created artists ordered the natural world in order to speak the truest of truth:

> The heavens declare the glory of God,
>   and the sky above proclaims his handiwork.
> Day to day pours out speech,
>   and night to night reveals knowledge.
> There is no speech, nor are there words,
>   whose voice is not heard.
> Their voice goes out through all the earth,
>   and their words to the end of the world.

In them he has set a tent for the sun,
  which comes out like a bridegroom leaving his
  chamber,
  and, like a strong man, runs its course with joy.
  (Ps. 19:1–5)

In the scope of time, the earth was once a newborn, birthed by God, perfect and lovely. The Artist imagined what could be and then spoke it into existence, casting light from darkness and day from night. Mountains, stretching tall and wide, appeared from the mind of God. Oceans deep filled the earth, marching up to the drawn line on the sand and no farther. And then, with great joy, as a father might seek his child's smile, God hid treasures for future discovery, delights so small and yet so complex the hunt for them would endure for millennia: the atom, DNA, the laws of math and physics, ingredients for medicine, hundreds of species, chocolate.

Man and woman, soon to come, could not miss the grandeur of such things.

Why? Why did he go to so much trouble? Why set into motion something so big and wild and, as we shall see, able to morph into something completely different than anything he originally intended?

Because he had something to say—or perhaps even more, something to *sing*.

Isn't that what artists do—communicate?

The manatees, the sound of bumblebees buzzing, the crispness of a carrot plucked from the ground—everything created conveys who God is and what he's like. The mountains tell us that he is incomprehensibly majestic, a rock, unchanging. The sparrow perched in her nest on those mountains—why was she made? Her message is that God sees all, even the smallest one, and, just as she cares for her young, his wings are a refuge for his own. The oceans, waves crashing on repeat—what is their song? He is living and active, and his ways, in their entirety, are vast and unsearchable. The storm gathering over those oceans, raging with thunder and lightning? God is all-powerful, mighty and sovereign.

All of creation combined at its birth to cry out: there is a God and he is gloriously beautiful.

For a moment, this creation held its breath, listening for the cosmic drumroll as God created and revealed his crowning glory: man and woman. God determined they would be the artistry most resembling him. They were most like his autobiography, his self-portrait. They were relational and communal, thinking and feeling, themselves able to create. They were given the ability to sing. They were designed with an ingrained desire to know and participate in intangible beauty: love, friendship, contentment, peace, and thankfulness. They were not only designed to reflect their Creator; they were designed to *worship* their Creator in their reflection of him.

God loosed them to search and seek treasure, implanted with hearts compelling them to do so. This is perhaps the most salient truth the created human being communicates: we are explorers and treasure seekers, which means there is a Treasure, an end to our searching and seeking.

In other words, there is a God and he is beautiful.

A Time to Die

And then the created mutinied against their Creator, rejecting what the natural world and their very own existence spoke of so clearly. There is a God? *Perhaps he is not what we thought;* *perhaps we are the true gods.* He is beautiful? *Perhaps we know better how to define what is beautiful and good.*

> Although they knew God, they did not honor him as God or give thanks to him, but they became futile in their thinking, and their foolish hearts were darkened. Claiming to be wise, they became fools, and exchanged the glory of the immortal God for images resembling mortal man and birds and animals and creeping things. (Rom. 1:21–23)

Spiritual death came after they questioned, "Did God actually say . . . ?" They experienced a sudden distance in their relationship with God, the weight of sin's curse, the shame of having marred perfect beauty and being wholly unable to rectify it.

There would be physical death as well—a time to die. This would be the necessary wage for their sin against God, but it was also a severe mercy and welcome reprieve. They wouldn't have to live in a corrupted world with corrupted hearts forever.

This first rejection of God led to more, for every human born has followed Adam and Eve to their destruction. Like them, we are no longer content to create in honor of the Creator; we use our creativity to invent ways of doing evil.[1] We take creation—meant to speak of God as clues on our treasure map—and make it our god.[2] We exchange the truth about God—that he exists and is beautiful—for the lie that we, and what we can create for ourselves, are the most beautiful.

We took a knife through God's canvas, a sledgehammer to his sculpture, a foolish and misguided red editing pen to his spoken words.

We thought we'd find life and beauty in doing so, but we've only found ugliness, suffering, pain, brokenness, and death ever since.

The newborn purity of the world has gone, leaving a brittle, broken, and decaying earth in its old age. Birth and death happen to us; their occurrences and specifics are entirely out of our control. From dust we came and to dust we will return; we take a stab at work and merrymaking in between. The fruit now spoils, the heart now grows cynical and distraught, the predator now devours its prey. The deceiving Serpent stretches his reach across the earth—stealing, killing, and destroying. Winter's death.

And, oh, the chill of winter.

In the middle of January, the days are short; pitch-black darkness descends before I've even finished preparing dinner. The heater kicks on often, and on the days when I can't escape the chill, I stand over the floor grates and feel the warm air pushing up through my wool socks. The excitement over rediscovering the new scarf I tucked away the previous winter has long waned, the overcast days and bare trees fill me with hunger for the sun and for color, and it's difficult in the morning to leave the cozy confines of my bed for the cold, tiled bathroom. Aside from the orange flames in the fireplace, winter is brown and dreary and seems to last far too long. In early March, I will stand at the kitchen window, feet on the floor grate, searching for signs of spring.

Our souls know this life, a hand-me-down from Adam and Eve, as a type of winter, as a searching and even groaning for spring. We long for release from barrenness; we long for growth and renewal when all we see around us is death.

Last fall, with winter coming on the horizon, I collapsed in tears in my closet. One moment I'd been putting away clean laundry and the next I was on my knees, crying for reasons I couldn't understand. My body felt heavy, my tears uncontrollable, because I was weary, the kind of weariness you feel in your bones. My life, in perpetual motion, came to a crashing halt—against a wall it felt—and my heart cracked on impact. Spilling out through its cracks were thought patterns and beliefs I hadn't known were there—thoughts and beliefs that had taken me on travels so far from peace and rest I'd forgotten my true home. Echoes of Adam and Eve's uttered words had passed from my own lips: *Perhaps I am my own god. Perhaps I know better what is beautiful and good.*

Suddenly, in pieces on the ground, I could see it all for what it was. A type of spiritual death had come, and I'd made the wreckage myself. I'd believed I was a messiah, a savior. I'd believed keeping people happy was primary; I'd fashioned them into my created gods. I'd believed I needed to be strong at all times and without physical limits, as only God himself is. At the realization that my life had become joyless, I sobbed tears onto the closet floor.

I'd lost sight of beauty.

For the days following, I couldn't seem to find it. The wall I'd hit reminded me of the blinding of the apostle Paul; I, too, felt as if I was walking around sightless. Something dramatic had occurred but I couldn't yet see what it was. In that darkness, I felt despair over the state of my soul. I felt deserted by God, for no truth comforted, no Ananias gave words to my experience.

I wondered if I was going crazy.

I am not alone in my winter. All of us, at some point in our lives, come to a place where the reality of our existence is so stark, so dark, we wonder if we'll ever know joy again. It feels like it's a time for the soul to die.

Must this be the depth to which Adam and Eve fell after knowing perfect contentment? The ground under them must have groaned as sin infected all of creation. We, too, as products of that infestation, live with similar groaning.

We know what winter can do, for we know death deep in our bones.

Leftover Hope

And yet, even Adam and Eve, if they'd looked close enough, could've seen a hint of light, of hope. If we look to time past, we can see it too.

Edith Schaeffer draws our eyes to its glimmer:

> Those who believe there is a God, and believe the Bible to be true, often leave out one important fact: that although creation and man have been spoiled by sin, there is left over in creation a glimpse of what God created in the first place. First, there remains the beauty of the whole universe, and of the heavens . . . so we can look out and see something that still declares His glory to us, even though sin has entered the world. We look at the trees and the mountains. We look at lakes and the variety of old oaks and evergreen trees, redwoods and weeping willows, and we see remnants of His creation which have not been spoiled . . . there are fragments of beauty to show the glory of the Creator, the Artist God.[3]

As a spry old woman's eyes sparkle with youth, some of God's perfect newborn creation still exists and, more importantly, still speaks.

I go with my children to the mountains butting up to my house. We traipse down rows of apple trees in the orchards on the side of the hill, stepping over rotting fruit that has fallen and standing on tiptoe to reach the ripest apples still hanging on the branches. We lose one another easily in the maze of Granny Smiths and Galas and, while I search for boys who have run up ahead, the sun beats hot on the back of my neck. I stop and look around. In that moment I am alone, taking in the view of the city stretching out below me and tracing the outline of the trees encircling me. Their limbs are like arms raised to the sky, perhaps pointing, perhaps inviting rain, and most certainly worshiping the Creator. *Look up and see*, they say, waving and rustling in the fall breeze.

I go to the Natural History Museum at the Smithsonian in Washington, DC, and I sit to watch a film with my youngest child about the fish recently discovered swimming at the bottom of the farthest ocean floor. Living at depths previously unexplored by man, they are awash in blinking pink and blue neon colors. I giggle to myself, suddenly in on the joke. A treasure hidden long ago, for all these years known only by God, each fish blinking and flashing for his pleasure alone. *Look and see*, they say, and then they prod: *go and seek*.

Though we are wretched in our sin and creation groans under the burden, the residual beauty speaks just as it did at the dawn of time. All of it still speaks about God—he exists, he is powerful, he is active, and he is beautiful. Even the decay of our groaning world communicates about him. Fall turning to winter: death comes for each of us. Winter itself: a large portion of life is waiting by faith. Winter turning to spring: there is a very real hope for new life after death.

There is a time for death, but there is also a time for birth. Our hearts, though heavy, need not despair.

We, too, are residual beauty from the beginning. The design of our physical bodies—just our skin alone, without seam or hem and able to renew itself in time—tells of our first parents. Our hearts, though sickened and shriveled by sin, are locked in a time when creation was not yet marred—we are beauty seekers and beauty creators as Adam and Eve were. We still carry in ourselves the image of God, and our creativity and search for unseen realities still compel us forward.

Creation, in other words, began the persistent drumbeat that continues to this day. We must bend our ears to hear what it speaks of God, especially as we endure this long, cold winter.

The lizard with severed tail able to grow a new one, a sea star with severed arm able to regenerate what was lost, a forest taken out by fire able to start anew, a body that has lost blood able to restore its supply. What do these natural occurrences say to each of us who come with bended ear? *God is still creating beauty.* In fact, he is creating now a beauty that didn't exist at the earth's birth but that only began after Adam and Eve's devastating decision. It is the beauty of redemption, and because God is still creating, he is at this very moment weaving this beauty in us.

What a thought. God is currently revealing his greatest artistic accomplishment, and we ourselves are the medium. *Are we seeking?*

If we're seeking, we know death remains with us, and not just with us but haunting us, oppressing us, stalking us, piercing us. Like Adam and Eve, we cannot escape our time to die.

However, might the first death be another glimmer of light, of hope, to those of us in perpetual winter who are seeking spring? For before Adam and Eve grew old and died after years of working the cursed ground and experiencing painful childbirth, before Cain killed his brother, even before the Garden gate closed, there was a first death. God slaughtered an innocent animal and made clothing for Adam and Eve's nakedness. Their spiritual deaths, bloated by shame, were mercifully covered by this physical sacrifice.

The innocent animal's death demonstrated the very first promise, made, strangely enough, to the Serpent but in earshot of those who needed to hear it most: "I will put enmity between you and the woman, and between your offspring and her offspring; he shall bruise your head, and you shall bruise his heel."[4]

God planted a seed in their minds that there would, in fact, be a Seed to come.

We can look back at this and see it all so clearly—it's the first scene in the story of beautiful redemption. Adam and Eve marred perfect beauty, but God refused to give up on them. He is a God who enters in and who will not let the story of us end with sin, with winter, and especially not with death. When we look back, we also see something important: he did not write the story quickly or hastily; the most beautiful beauty is never immediate. We look back and see that he made space for faith. We look back and realize we might not actually recognize beauty if it weren't contrasted by pain.

Because of Adam and Eve, the treasures hidden by God may be buried deeper than before, secreted away under darkness, but they are there nonetheless, waiting for those who are treasure seekers.

All may seem lost, but, in fact, the past tells us there is unfolding beauty to behold in the present, beauty that will send us to our knees with arms raised like the apple trees: if there is a time to die, there will be a time of rebirth as well.

I discovered this myself after a few days of unexplainable tears, of giving myself to physical rest and crying out to God in repentance and sorrow over where I'd traveled. I recognized that the wall I'd run into had been put there by God himself. He hadn't deserted me at all; he loved me enough to carefully restore my joy. He also wanted me to know his beauty once again and how much he wanted to create new beauty in me. To get there, I would need to engage the process—the painful, wringing process of repentance and change. From death to new life.

I clung to the belief that God can bring beauty from the ashes, that my faith and obedience could be the soil from which he would one day produce pleasant fruit.

Mostly, I clung to the belief that God is the Artist-Creator, writing the beauty of redemption in my life.

All my other hopes had shattered, but this one remained.

Look Up, Oh Heart

The wind calls out, rustling the leaves that have fallen off the trees and blowing around the corners of the house. The tree roots in the forest interconnect below the surface, miraculously feeding one another. Heat waves from the sun pound on our skin, revealing themselves through sunburns. All unseen things, all continually at work.

Because all things, visible and invisible, were created by him and for him,[5] the invisible things shout as loudly as the visible. Listen closely and you will hear what they speak about God, and, therefore, what he speaks about you. God is sovereign over and active in the unseen places—in your soul, in your relationships, in your future. God is able to make all things new and, with the broken pieces of your life, he can make something beautiful too. In fact, that has been his plan all along.

We can be uncaged from fear, even the fear of death.

We can be rescued from despair and hopelessness.

We can be redefined, not by our past but by our future.

God sings to us through his creation—he is there, he is beautiful, and he is still creating beauty—so that our hearts will sing in hope-filled response to him.

Look up, oh heart, look up. Stand at the kitchen window and search for signs of life, listening to creation's song, the drumbeat of redemption Adam and Eve heard and that the prophets after them put lyrics to: "Behold, I am doing a new thing; now it springs forth, do you not perceive it? I will make a way in the wilderness and rivers in the desert" (Isa. 43:19).

As it turns out, the seed of their hope—and ours—was nestled underground all along.

Unexpected Beauty

For everything there is a season, and a time for
every matter under heaven: *a time to plant, and
a time to pluck up what is planted.*

S OMETIMES MY LIFE doesn't make sense to me. When I
step back and look at myself through my neighbors' eyes
or through the filter of cultural values, I seem crazy even to
myself, because I believe there is an invisible God who created this world, who created me (and every other person),
and who has authority over what he's created. Even though
I've never seen this God, I love him. My entire world is based
upon this truth that God exists and that he is beautiful and
that he's turning all things to reflect his beauty. I'm all-in
on this bet. My relationships, my money, my marriage, my
decisions, my work, my time, my ministry, my dreams and

hopes—all of it's out there on the table, betting on a promise. And even I have moments of doubt: What if it's not true or what if it's only partially true?

When trials send me ricocheting through various emotions, it can be challenging to remain steady in faith, because going all-in with an invisible God doesn't make life suddenly all roses and unicorns. And this life of faith requires that I set aside all rights to myself and teaches me to wait for all things to be made beautiful based upon some promises made long ago.

That may sound foolish to some, and certainly God has asked me to do things that, outside of his promises, appear crazy. For one, we packed up our family and moved across the country to plant a church in a city where we didn't know a soul. Everyone asked us "How will you get paid?" and "How exactly do you start a church?" and we had no good answers. In our new city, no one much cared that we were there. When we cheerily explained to our aforementioned neighbors why we'd moved in next door, they stared at us, speechless, as if we were aliens from another planet.

Ironically, that is just what we are.

People have been staring at promise-believers for millennia, starting with Noah. I wonder what his friends and family members thought of him. I wonder if he hoped no one would notice the great big boat being constructed in his yard. I wonder how many doubts he harbored as he hammered one more nail into one more plank of wood with nary a drop of rain in sight. I wonder if he'd already considered the cost before he began building the ark and, after he began, I wonder if obedience was worth it to him. It must have been, because he went all-in on a command and a promise—even literally all-in when he boarded the ark alongside a bunch of smelly animals.

After Noah came the prophets, a motley cast of characters, tasked by God to do downright weird things. I wonder what Ezekiel was thinking for the 390 days he lay on his side out in the city for everyone to see, acting out the coming siege of Jerusalem with bricks and iron griddles. I wonder if he felt foolish or frustrated that God was calling him to suffer for a bunch of people who weren't listening and didn't seem to care. Apparently not, because he went all-in on a command and a promise.

The prophets were the Israelites' conscience, beacons of light throughout generations of darkness, but everyone thought they were crazy because they staked everything, even their physical lives, on a couple of ancient promises God had made to their forefather, Abraham, about a seed. They believed God and believed he was beautiful and believed he would make something out of all their national rubble and anguish. They tried to get everyone around them to go all-in on this promise.

And they were proven right. Absolutely 100 percent right.

Everyone who walked by Ezekiel and thought he was crazy, lying there on the ground? Everyone who ignored the promises, grappled for any immediate beauty they could find, and resisted the idea of God in order that they might live how they wanted? They were wrong, and it cost them dearly.

God is unexpected in so many ways, and he does unexpected things through people who go all-in on a command and a promise.

This gives me hope, and above all else it teaches me that his promises can be trusted. If the prophets, who had so little to go on, believed God, I can too, even when God is unexpected and his plan sends me through surprising twists and turns.

I don't like the unexpected. I prefer hedging my bets with a plan B, not having to go all-in on a promise by faith. I want to figure it all out. I want to understand the plan of God from beginning to end. I want a guarantee there will at least be significance and meaning in my suffering. My heart demands predictable answers from an unexpected God.

But he simply holds out his promises. That's what we see when we peer into the past: every time, he asks people to go all-in with obedience and trust, on a command and a promise.

This is why beauty is so often hard to see in life: it's easier to walk away to a visible plan B, and waiting makes us weary. The crazy person who actually has hope in this cynical, hardened world often stands, builds, or proclaims alone. And what if God chooses to show us how he makes all things beautiful through loss and suffering? What if trusting him means obedience that costs our pleasure and comfort and makes us look a little bit crazy?

And yet we cannot ignore the siren song of beauty filtering through what we see in the natural world and what we read in papyrus pages. If we're attuned to it, the song ignites something in us and compels us, as a seed sprouting in our hearts, to seek the light, to seek out the unseen realities of the universe and find our place in them.

There is something inside of us that *knows* there are truths bigger than us. That's because the invisible God himself has planted a seed in each of us—a sense of eternity in our hearts.[1] Our awareness of the seed is limited and foggy but it is there, calling us to seek and search out what lies beneath the surface. It whispers through our heartache when we ask,

"Is this all there is?" It murmurs when we question, "How could such evil exist on this planet?" And it shouts through the joy of experiencing love and renewal, "There is beauty bigger than you're able to behold in one life."

When we cultivate the implanted seed, we discover it craves a conclusion of significance, truth, and meaning, as if it's a question mark, as if it's seeking something outside of itself, as if it seeks the fulfillment of a promise.

When God Is Silent, He Isn't Still

After Adam and Eve and generations after them had come and gone, after the prophets grew quiet, winter and decaying old age descended upon the earth.

Frozen silence. Four hundred years of it, to be exact.

In silence, there is always more time to question, and I imagine the people who'd gone all-in on a promise did question. They were relatives of Adam and Eve, after all, and their unfulfilled expectations likely led them to question the unexpected God. Could God really have created this world? Could God really have planted the seed of eternity in our hearts? Is God still at work, or has he given up on us?

The Seed, hidden beneath layers of frozen winter ground and hardened hearts, lay waiting.

And then.

Time suddenly and inexplicably became full, ready to give birth, an invisible Seed becoming a visible sprout.

A promise had been given long ago, almost forgotten, although many had whispered of it after it was spoken, when they walked along the road and when they tucked their children in at night and when the natural world groaned with labor pains.

The promise had gone like this: Through your Seed all the nations shall be blessed.[2] God had said those words to Abraham so long ago that the silent generations must have thought it a myth.

We, too, know the kind of silence extending so long that we begin to question everything. We know the kind of pleading prayers that seemingly go unanswered. We know fallow ground and desperate barrenness.

And yet.

There'd been signs of pregnancy all along: examples and types of what had been promised, heralds and spokesmen, lone voices crying out to be heard who had instead been viciously silenced. Because who goes all-in on only a promise?

So much silence.

And waiting. Waiting upon waiting. Generations upon generations defined solely by waiting. For some, probably too much waiting on seemingly empty promises, too many sideways glances from neighbors.

Those with their ear to the ground, listening for the drumbeat, heard Habakkuk, one lone voice among the waiting, crying out in the night: "O LORD, how long shall I cry, and You will not hear?" (Hab. 1:2 NKJV).

Another, Jeremiah, wept, "Why do you forget us forever, why do you forsake us for so many days?" (Lam. 5:20).

Silence.

In the silence, violence. Plundering, strife, and iniquity prevailed. Perverse judgment proceeded. The waiting people suffered under their own impenitent hearts. *How long, O Lord?*

Surely, for those who were still listening for the drumbeat in the silence, God's original spoken promise must have echoed in their minds. They must have considered the voice of God's spokesman slicing through the noise of the world: "Look among the nations and watch—be utterly astounded! For I will work a work in your days which you would not believe, though it were told you" (Hab. 1:5 NKJV).

He begged them to go all-in on the promise.

And then, again, silence—generations of it. Physical eyes still saw the beauty of creation—it never stopped communicating, an anchor in the lull of time—but those eyes also saw the continued rise of strife and struggle. Physical ears likely heard evil screaming louder than any long-ago whispered promise, and anyway, no one other than God and Abraham had witnessed that promise.

The people grew tired of waiting; few were looking among the nations and watching, few were standing in the kitchen window searching for signs of spring. The whispered promise was almost forgotten.

But God never forgot.

The unexpected God was silent, save for the natural world and the implanted seed of eternity in hearts, but he'd been working all along, knitting in the womb of time. The consistency of the dawn and the ever-moving waves communicate about him: even when he is silent, he is not still.

Through the silent generations, with humankind none the wiser, his hands upended the world map, moving nations and world leaders as pawns on a chessboard.

He first raised the Babylonians to conquer and scatter his people, who in turn built synagogues in far-flung outposts. Then the Greeks rose to center stage, bringing with them a love for words and ideas and creating a common world language. Finally the Romans appeared and conquered the

49

known world, building roads and throwing open borders for easy travel.

Beauty was happening in the unseen. The Seed was preparing to sprout.

All of this took time—beauty always does—and no one could have guessed how God might use his own beloved people's sin and subsequent exilic suffering to create unbelievable beauty. *For I will work a work in your days which you would not believe, though it were told you.*

Scattered promise-believers? Outpost synagogues where people gather to hear news and ideas? In a language all can understand? Brought by messengers through open borders and travelable roads?

Clues upon clues that God was preparing his most important speech.

In our own barrenness, in the unanswered prayer, we must know that God may be silent but he is never still.

The Ugly and the Beautiful

The womb of time grew heavy under God's steady hand.
And then.

"When the fullness of the time had come, God sent forth His Son" (Gal. 4:4 NKJV).

The womb of time burst open, and silence gave way to the Word. The cries from lone voices of long ago rang with truth, and their prophetic utterances fell, fulfilled, in quick succession—born of a virgin, a son of Bethlehem, wrapped in swaddling clothes.

Past and future beauty found their foundation and conclusion in that present moment.

Those who had ears to hear and eyes to see in that time nodded in recognition, whispering to one another, "What was it that God said to Abraham?" *In you—through your Seed—all the nations shall be blessed.*

And all who have acknowledged and cultivated the seed of eternity in their hearts, following its question mark in search of a conclusion, find it in the promised Seed. They also find the Truth and the Way and the Life in this Seed. He is the Word who spoke and who sings the song to our heart's cry for meaning and for eternal life. He is Jesus.

The Seed of Abraham came and, through his life, the winter that had lasted for centuries began to thaw.

The angels sang. The wise men sought. Mary pondered. And then.

He was hidden because Herod was hunting.

Silence again.

Waiting again, for the Seed-Son needed time to grow.

A lone voice in the vein of Elijah and Jeremiah called out into the silence, proclaiming to anyone who would listen that the kingdom of God was at hand. The conclusion their hearts—and ours—sought was at hand. God was about to communicate in a way he hadn't ever before. John urged them to take notice, to prepare themselves, to listen, to stand at the kitchen window and watch for the coming spring, to go all-in on the promise.

The water turned to wine. The fish and loaves multiplied. Crowds drew near to see. The Seed they saw sprouting up before them was so . . . *unexpected.* They'd come to see a politician with a winning smile and good ideas, an activist with strong arms and a fighting spirit decrying Rome, a leader with charisma the Jewish community could be proud of. Instead they found him unattractive and disappointing, because they were looking for immediate beauty rather than the promise from long ago: "For [Jesus] grew up before [the Father] like a young plant, and like a root out of dry ground; he had no form or majesty that we should look at him, and no beauty that we should desire him" (Isa. 53:2).

The prophet's promise had come true: Jesus wasn't outwardly beautiful.

And then the Word started speaking, and his words astonished and confounded them far more than his appearance. The Word's words, the very words of God, were so . . . *unexpected*. He not only appeared physically unattractive but his words were directed to the downtrodden, the beaten-up, the despairing, and the hopeless, not to the beautiful people. The wait-ers, the promise-believers always hear the beauty first.

With astonishing authority, he looked them in the eye and said, "Blessed are the poor in spirit" (Matt. 5:3). He spoke to mourners, the meek and powerless, the persecuted, those who'd been hungering and thirsting for the hard, cold winter of sin within their hearts to turn pure and new. Those who stood at the kitchen window looking for signs of spring were surprised to not only see the promised Seed but to hear that they—the wait-ers, the promise-believers—were first in line for blessed beauty.

After inviting the poor and powerless to receive such beauty in the kingdom of God at hand, he told them how to get it: "Unless your righteousness exceeds that of the scribes and Pharisees, you will never enter the kingdom of heaven" (5:20). They must have immediately recoiled, for the scribes and Pharisees stood in stark contrast to the beautiful words alight in Jesus's mouth. The scribes and the Pharisees were the law's interpreters and enforcers, known for their prideful piety and exacting way with religious regulations. They'd taken the law given to Moses and, over centuries, added rule upon rule until they had squeezed out every ounce of joy and every ounce of God himself. To these legalists, the law was the end, the goal, the finish line, and all who tamed it could enter into blessing. The scribes and Pharisees offered no grace, no peace, no meaningful conclusion for the implanted seed's question; they only meted out judgment and religious bondage.

The crowds must have begun to worry as they listened to Jesus's words, sensing the promised beauty slipping away. They already knew from long trying that they could never completely do all that was in the law. The beauty of spring, moments before within their grasp, remained out of reach.

I imagine it was then that Jesus smiled and paused, giving them space to consider how incapable they were of such a feat, how the implanted seed cannot find its conclusion in itself. The drum mallet hung in the air and all of time stopped.

And then the beautiful song: "I have come to fulfill the law on your behalf."[3]

The drumbeat had all along been a heartbeat—the heartbeat of God pursuing beauty for his creation.

Did anyone in the crowd that day grasp the enormity of what Jesus was talking about?

The Seed had sprouted up through dry ground. It appeared that the old winter had gone; the new spring had come. It was a time to pluck up what had been planted—the law—and a time for the planted Seed to sprout and multiply.

For those who had eyes to see the Seed and ears to hear his heart beating like a drum, Jesus suddenly became the most beautiful person they'd ever encountered.

What Jesus Didn't Say

Jesus speaks the same words to us that he spoke to the crowd that day. To all of us who are waiting, all of us who are downtrodden, all of us who are mourning, he says, "Blessed are you." His attention is not directed toward the beautiful people who think they've perfected life or think they've found the conclusion in themselves. His loving eye is instead on the broken-down, the ones who know beyond all knowing how spiritually poverty-stricken they are. If that is you, he has so much to say, and it all begins with, "Blessed are you." Because the beauty of his grace and truth can richly fill the emptiness in your poverty.

However, if we were in the crowd that day, listening with astonishment to Jesus's words, I wonder if we'd have noticed what Jesus *didn't* say. Or, for that matter, what he didn't say or do throughout his whole life on earth. In place of the law, he planted a new, fruit-bearing seed—himself—but he left many things unstated and, more notably, unfixed. What he didn't say and do is perhaps equally as important as what he did say and do, especially for us in a day when we are once again waiting, and we tend to believe and convey that Jesus's chosen word, *blessed*, means he will solve our every problem and protect us from suffering.

Author Zack Eswine calls Jesus's unsaid and unfixed things "inconsolable things."

> "Inconsolable things" are the sins and miseries that will not be eradicated until heaven comes home, the things that only Jesus, and no one of us, can overcome. We cannot expect to change what Jesus has left unfixed for the moment.

This presence of inconsolable things reminds us that healing is not the same as heaven. Miracles are real and powerful, but they do not remove the inconsolable things. Those whose leprosy Jesus healed coughed again or skinned their elbows. Those who were blind but now able to see could still get a speck of burning sand stuck in their eye. The formerly lame could still fall and break their leg. Lazarus was raised from the dead only to find his resumed life filled with death threats. Moreover, the raised friend of Jesus would die again someday, along with this company of the healed. Bodily healing in this world is not heaven. Sickness and death are inconsolable things. Their healing reveals Jesus but does not remove sickness or death from life under the sun.[4]

We cannot expect to change what Jesus has left unfixed for the moment.

For us, centuries removed from that crowd, this means we, too, must go all-in on the promise—believing all things will one day be made beautiful—while very much living in the midst of terrible suffering. We must recognize the Seed as evidence and proof that God is a promise-keeping God. We must know the invisible God and the not-yet-fulfilled promise more intimately than the reality of our trials.

We cannot expect to change what Jesus has left unfixed for the moment.

I've lived practically my entire life trying to disprove that statement. I've obsessed over perfection like a child attempts over and over to build a tall block tower only to watch it fall each time.

If I just try harder this time . . .

If I just use a little more willpower . . .

If I am more exacting with my work . . .

If I take more control . . .

If I finally figure out what will produce the results I'm looking for . . .

If I just do a little bit more . . .

If I can just figure out what it is that God has called me to do . . .

If I pray harder or have more faith . . .

If I can only accomplish all that I've set out to do . . .

If I can finally get my life in order . . .

What, then? What is the conclusion I'm looking for, exactly?

Well, in my mind, I'd experience peace, satisfaction, and joy. I'd finally reach the pinnacle. Everything about my life would be brought into order, including my marriage, my children, and my own mind and heart. More importantly, I'd avoid experiencing longing, unfulfilled dreams, pain, loneliness, disappointment, or failure. Somehow, if I can fix it all, I might be able to bypass what I've seen others walk through: betrayal, depression, cancer, prodigal children.

In my obsession with perfection, I can pretend inconsolable things aren't there.

I can earn my blessing.

I once heard of a pastor who spent time each week on a farm pulling weeds, hoping to bring about the renewal of all things on this earth. There is a reason he had to go back each week. The weeds kept growing back, because the weeds are always with us.

And my weeds are always going to be with me, just as yours are always going to be with you. To believe otherwise is to believe according to the law, a dead stalk in dry ground that tells us we're able to fix inconsolable things ourselves, that perfection on earth is possible. These are words of death, although often rather than sounding like death they sound like a noble dream. These are beliefs, however, that remove us from Jesus's fixed attention, beliefs that purposefully set him aside and force us to look inside of ourselves for the hope and power we need for living. We become the answer unto ourselves.

Jesus did address this, remember. He said these are the ways—the ancient ways—humanity has tried to eradicate sin and seek the conclusion their implanted heart-seed seeks—peace with God. He said the only true conclusion is *gifted* blessing, *gifted* peace, *gifted* power, and *gifted* faith. *Gifted* means it comes from someone else. He said that someone else was himself. He does it all for us according to our faith, but we have to wait to see with our eyes the completion and fullness of the blessing.

It is often an affront to us that Jesus left inconsolable things, that in his goodness he asks us to wait on the promise while also enduring pain and suffering. We often find it offensive that he asks for us to go all-in in the form of obedience that is hard and self-sacrificing. We stamp our feet and question how anything beautiful could be made from our suffering. We much prefer the pursuit of beauty we can grab onto in the present: immediately satisfying things. Jesus doesn't offer consolation to what cannot truly be consoled in the present; the world, however, will offer this false comfort.

Among the crowds, Jesus warned his listeners about this very thing. He described himself as a seed sower and his words as the seeds. There will be some, he said, who hear his words but don't actually listen and still others who listen but then fall away, either because of suffering or because they are drawn away by the world's offerings of false riches.[5]

Our perpetual problem is that we don't know true beauty when it is right in front of us. In our definition, beauty means no negativity, no suffering, no longing, and no waiting. Beauty is, in other words, instant and consumable.

We must be careful what we call beautiful. We must be careful not to attribute words to the Word that he never said. If picking weeds is our hope, then we have none at all. If we demand the present be perfectly beautiful, we not only prove we weren't actually listening to Jesus's words but we become deeply offended that God is not living up to what we thought he'd be.

But as we look to time past, the inconsolable things communicate to us that there is still time to come and still creating left to do, and that there is an important element of waiting and faith involved in getting to see and experience ultimate beauty. Following Jesus still means going all-in on commands and promises.

We are not meant to be completely fulfilled on this earth. This is a beauty held out by the world. It is shiny and sounds good, and we believe if God really loved us he would fulfill us completely in the here and now.

But that's not what Jesus said. Dear heart, Jesus didn't say he'd save you from affliction. Instead he asked you to go all-in on a promise of unexpected beauty sprouting up through that very affliction. He asks you to shift your eyes from tangible pain to an invisible hope.

Do we still think he is the most beautiful person we've ever encountered?

Life through Death

The crowds pressed in on him, trying to knit him according to their desires. He fled them, knowing their expectations and that the time was premature.

John, in prison, sent men to Jesus with one question: "Are You the Coming One, or do we look for another?" (Matt. 11:3 NKJV).

Violence, plundering, strife, and iniquity prevailed. Perverse judgment proceeded. The waiting people still suffered. *How long, O Lord?*

But God was knitting in the womb of time. The labor pains grew increasingly intense; those who had eyes to see and ears to hear followed them closely. Jesus vocalized what was to be birthed next: "I came that you might have life."[6]

He was about to demonstrate how true life is born—through death.

Because only a seed that gives itself to be broken open lives again and bears much fruit.

Beauty We Want to Avoid

For everything there is a season, and a time for every matter under heaven: *a time to kill, and a time to heal.*

HOWEVER ODD IT MIGHT SEEM to my neighbors and even to myself at times, I have gone all-in with this Jesus. I have crawled up on an altar like a compliant Isaac, choosing to be a living sacrifice wafting like incense to please my Creator. My life is no longer my own.

At least that's what I say.

My deeper-held hopes betray me. In the string of weary, monotonous days, or when I'm wading deep in problems, I daydream that there will one day soon be a finish line to my sacrifice, that I will eventually get my life back from the altar. The finish line sometimes aligns with retirement or the empty nest years, when I can finally lay down the baton of self-death—considering others more important than myself, sowing seeds of generosity, caring for the least of these, carrying the burdens and concerns of others, continually pouring my life out as a servant—and then finally become free. Free to come alive to my own wants and desires, free to become my own master.

If I'm honest, I believe God owes me this finish line where I can get my life back, as if sacrifice is a paid job rather than a way of life. As if I'm still alive to myself rather than dead to self and alive to God.

Surely there is a way around sacrifice.

I am determined to find it. I *expect* to find it.

The crowds gathered around Jesus in Jerusalem at the height of Passover, waving palm branches with similar expectations, but what they *saw* confused them more than anything he'd ever *said* to them. The people called, with their shouts, for him to take up his mantle of earthly kingship, but rather than appearing before them on a noble horse, he came with legs dangling awkwardly off a lowly donkey as it trudged through town. This? This was the Seed who God promised Abraham would bless all nations?

Even his closest friends were confounded as, later that week, they watched him kneel in the dirt to wash feet as the lowliest servant was expected to do.

Perhaps they were confounded because they, too, hadn't actually listened. They'd traveled with him and eaten meals with him for years, but their expectations and lack of understanding must have muffled his words. It wasn't just his friends who'd misunderstood; the Word's words had been ignored, twisted, and attacked by those with influence and power. All who heard him, it seemed, listened for what they'd wanted to hear, refusing what he'd been saying all along: there would be no earthly kingdom and there would be no toppling of Roman rule.

There would only be death.

Jesus reprimanded his own friend for thinking the kingdom of God meant avoiding pain and death.

> From that time Jesus began to show his disciples that he must go to Jerusalem and suffer many things from the elders and chief priests and scribes, and be killed, and on the third day be raised. And Peter took him aside and began to rebuke him, saying, "Far be it from you, Lord! This shall never happen to you." But he turned and said to Peter, "Get behind me, Satan! You are a hindrance to me. For you are not setting your mind on the things of God, but on the things of man." (Matt. 16:21–23)

Perhaps this is what the prophet Habakkuk meant when he said, "For I am doing a work in your days that you would not believe if told" (1:5).

So few had eyes to see; so few had ears to hear.

Are you the Coming One, or do we look for another?

One by one, his closest friends turned away, having misunderstood the whispered promise, looking for another; to death he went alone.

Enraged by their unmet expectations of who he should've been and what he should've done, filled with hatred knowing they could not mold him into their own image, the crowd—the created—killed their Creator.

After his body had been laid out on a slab and light in the tomb sealed off with a stone, Jesus's friends, as all grievers do, must have thought back over his life and all that they'd seen him do and heard him say, trying to make sense of it. The theme of his words and life had certainly been the kingdom of God; he'd talked about it constantly, using parables and word pictures to describe what it was like, saying first and foremost that it was "at hand."[1]

If the kingdom of God had been at hand, it appeared to have been stopped in its tracks, sputtering to an abrupt halt before gaining any momentum at all. How could this be? Perhaps they'd followed a charlatan rather than the Messiah. Surely the kingdom of God, valuing love, righteousness, and beauty above all, would not allow its supreme ruler to suffer through brutality, betrayal, and a broken body.

And yet he'd been brutally killed on a cross, finalized by a spear.

Silence and grief. Waiting and helplessness. Scattering and sorrow.

However, there was something else none of them yet understood: Jesus had *allowed* himself to die. He'd willingly given his life into hands he'd created, to die for the very ones who'd driven the stakes through his body. He demonstrated that the secret of the kingdom of God lay in the seed: *to have true life, one must first lay it down*. In Jesus's case, he chose to *give away* true life by laying his down.

Life through death, beauty through scars—this is the kingdom of God that was "at hand" and is still at hand this current day, made possible by the Seed breaking open. The kingdom Jesus invited us into remains a kingdom of paradox, where what seems self-contradictory or absurd in reality expresses what is absolutely true.[2]

The last shall be first.

The lowliest are the greatest.

The free willingly become slaves.

The weak are actually strong.

The poor in spirit are rich.

The humble are exalted.

Those who give, receive.

The ones who lose all, gain all.

And the seed at the core of the kingdom: those who die are the ones who truly live.

Christ, the ruler of this kingdom, embodied paradox. He had no beauty that people should desire him but he also expressed the glorious beauty of God in his perfect life and sacrifice.[3] He proved that the one who dies, who gives his life away, is the one who actually comes to life and multiplies himself.

Likewise for us, suffering and death hold no outward beauty that we should embrace them but are the way to character, joy, and eternal life. "We rejoice in our sufferings, knowing that suffering produces endurance, and endurance produces character, and character produces hope, and hope does not put us to shame" (Rom. 5:3–5).

The question remains: Do we believe this? Do we believe this enough to *want* a place in the kingdom of God?

To embrace Christ and to become a citizen of his kingdom is to live by paradox: we must embrace weakness to be made strong, we must serve in order to receive, we must live in the world while holding citizenship in another, we must suffer persecution as more than conquerors, we must die to ourselves daily in order to live, and we must look at every-thing difficult and painful as something that will eventually be made into good.

To desire and know true beauty in life, to understand how God can make all things beautiful in time, is to cleave ourselves to these paradoxes.

There is beauty in paradox, as there is beauty in contrast.

I go to the Louvre in Paris and crane my head above the crowd in order to glimpse the *Mona Lisa*. Every plaque and description is in French, a language I don't speak, but I need only my eyes to understand her smirk. Although she is not herself beautiful, the painting draws the eye because of Leo-nardo da Vinci's use of contrast between light and dark.

Vermeer did the same with light and dark in his famous painting *Girl with a Pearl Earring*, as did Van Gogh in *Starry Night*. Claude Monet used more color but still brought beauty through the contrast colors of orange and blue.

Artists use contrast to create beauty, and God, the great Artist, is no different. In the contrasts of life, we find that bitter can somehow become sweet.

The hours and sometimes days of pain during childbirth give way to one of the most memorable and joy-filled mo-ments: the first minutes of a newborn baby's life—its cry piercing the air, the feel of its fresh skin against our own. Think of the contrast: a miracle bringing pure joy through unspeakable pain.

The grief of watching a loved one die from cancer and then going on without her—what beauty could possibly come from helplessly observing a long and arduous dying process? In those moments, we are given an opportunity to see the worst stuff life has to offer: the grittiness and ugliness and awfulness of life. All insignificant things fall away, and, if we see with eyes of faith, our hope can become so sure in those moments that it's as if we're in a boat attached to an anchor in the middle of a tempestuous sea. Think of the contrast: a steadfast hope solidified through crumbling.

The testing various trials bring, unwanted life circumstances, the unexpected twists and turns—these, too, can be beautiful, because through these occurrences come strong character, endurance, godly wisdom, and comfort with which we can then comfort others.

Through trials, our faith increases.

Through broken hearts, we get the nearness of God.

Through failure, we experience redemption.

Through death, those in Christ get heaven.

We want the beauty of hope, life, and transformation; we just don't want them in the way they come. But perhaps this is the very reason Jesus left us with inconsolable things—he wants to give us blessing upon blessing.

Could it be that we've spent our whole lives avoiding beauty?

All of the Bitter, None of the Sweet

I find myself among the crowd, trying to see what has happened to Jesus's body, trying to understand his death. As the Word's last words ring in my mind, however, I am like a child, covering my ears and humming. None of this makes sense; this kingdom seems absurd. These are horrible things—death, disconcerting trials, hurts and scars. These are things that change the scope of lives. How could death be the way to beauty?

Everything in me tells me to run as Peter did, to avoid grief and pain, to escape suffering, to fear death, to not associate myself with this Seed-Son. Everything in me urges my return to the madding crowd, where I can wave palm branches over my expectations and hope beyond hope that true life and glorious beauty might come through more sensible things: power, influence, money, youth, comfort, entertainment, or a seamless life. Anything but pain and suffering.

With Life in death's grave, I try to disarm the paradox.

Sometimes I'm invited to disarm through subtle whispers of doubt: *This is all there is. This is the end of it all; there is nothing of value beyond this life. Get what you can get now. Take what will satisfy you in this moment.* Essentially, I want to disarm the paradox by chasing ugly beauty, because it makes more sense to me. But I know now that ugly beauty is deceitful beauty; eventually it will lead me to darkness, emptiness, and decay. I've sampled and even devoured whole the fruits of selfish ambition, pride, fantasy, bitterness, envy, and hatred. At first bite they tasted sweet and satisfying but soon after turned bitter and rotten, poisoning me. As soon as I reached out to touch the seductive fruit in order that I might possess it, ugly beauty morphed into only ugliness. All of the bitter, none of the sweet.

We'd think ugly beauty might be spotted more easily, that we'd not be tricked so handily, but I am deceived constantly. I move about my house, hanging curtains, adjusting blinds, arranging wreaths, and lighting candles because, as I told you before, I enjoy creating warm physical environments. I love bright colors, lit lamps, and sentimental keepsakes, but what I really love, if you want to know the truth, is *order*. If everything is in its place, straightened and fluffed, my world feels right. I'm not a crazy person about it—but okay, yes I am. And also? I have three boys—one of whom is a teenager—who don't care one single bit about having a beautiful home. As long as heaps of food appear on the dinner table, they couldn't care less if a decorative pillow falls to the ground and gets shoved under the couch and covered in dust bunnies. Why bother with a napkin when you can wipe your Cheetos fingerprints on the couch cushion? This is what I live with.

It's not a problem that I love beauty and attempt to make my home beautiful; it's a problem when I chase order to the point of perfection. When we moved into our home, it needed a ton of work, and we didn't have the money to do it all at once. So I started a list, a dream really, of all I hoped to change in my home over time. I couldn't wait to get everything just the way I wanted it.

Slowly, my husband and I chipped away at my list. When we updated our dining room, I absolutely loved it, but then I turned around and saw my kitchen, drooping with age, and suddenly the joy of a beautiful dining room withered into dissatisfaction.

At various times, chasing ugly beauty in the form of a picture-perfect home has made me crazy with my children, discontented to my husband, and greedy for money to put toward making my dream a reality. I tell myself that one day I'll have the house just as I want it, but I *know* this desire is a fruit, once devoured, that will poison me. Jesus said we'll always have the poor among us, and I'm pretty sure I'll always have Cheetos fingerprints on my couch as well.

I need to remember this, because I so easily forget: I will never get everything in my life perfectly arranged. Everything will not be made right in this life. I won't ever reach a magical moment when I finally feel enough, as if this is the end of the story. I'm going to have loose ends. No matter how hard I try to make it so, beauty that decays is not true beauty; it won't disarm the paradox. It won't protect me from suffering.

How about you? Are you chasing the seductive beauty of the harlot who is leading you to your destruction? Are you actively pursuing the fleeting physical beauty of youth or a certain weight on the scale? Are you worshiping the creature or the creation, wanting only what you can see and touch?

We must remember that the created killed the Creator, and created things put in the Creator's place will kill us too. Jesus died that ugly death, taking on all of our desires and pursuits of ugly beauty so that we might experience the fruitful and lasting beauty of righteousness. We either, according to the kingdom paradox, die to ourselves and live, or we seek ugly beauty and give our lives over to sin and all its bitter fruit. All the bitter, none of the sweet.

Before he died, Jesus tried to tell his disciples and he tries to tell us: the kingdom of God is beautiful in its paradox. It speaks to how things *really are*, not how we wish they were.

Life through death, beauty through scars, finding life through letting it go.

I don't want to believe it.

John's words echo in my own heart: *Are you the Coming One, or do we look for another?*

A Time for Healing

Life and beauty do come through death. Jesus not only said so but he also proved it. When everyone questioned if he was the one they'd been waiting for, God answered with the resurrection. When Jesus's heart restarted, it was the drumbeat of time restarting in marching pursuit of each of us—for every one of us seeking hope and purpose in our pain. His heart beat again for the poor in spirit, the downtrodden in heart, the betrayed, and the wounded. There had been a time to kill but now that time was over. Now would come a time to heal.

Think of the paradox: God gave himself, knowing we would kill him, but was wise and powerful enough to turn that sin into our salvation.

The death and resurrection of Christ was and is our healing, because in fulfilling what he said he'd do, he showed us that the gospel is true. If God can defeat death, there is nothing he can't do, and there isn't anyone who remains out of his reach. This means he really *can* make all things beautiful in their time, including me and including you. "He hung . . . on the cross deformed, and His deformity is our beauty."[4] He is the source of our beauty because, in him, all things that are dead—physically and spiritually—can be made alive and forever healed. Good news, indeed.

Jesus's resurrection provided the true healing we all needed, but for this present time it hasn't and won't fix the inconsolable things. His resurrection, then, is an invitation to life in the paradoxical kingdom of God, where to follow Jesus is to embrace what doesn't make sense: faith in what we can't see, hope beyond what we can think or imagine, sacrificial love in imitation of someone who laid down his life for those who despised him. Christ initiated a kingdom of redemption—making all things beautiful in time—and this is the kingdom that will reign forever. We do well to chase his heartbeat.

The truth that Christ's kingdom will forever reign, when all things will be made beautiful and right, is *the* truth we need for our day. It's the truth that enables us to face discomfort, monotony, broken relationships, sickness, loss, and death with unwavering hands and steadfast hearts. It's the truth that enables us to *sing* in the face of uncertainty. It's the truth that motivates us to faithfully serve in obscurity. It's the truth that helps us hang in and hang on. Because of Christ's resurrection, we know that death will be the last enemy destroyed and we will once again walk with God as Adam and Eve did. Something good is guaranteed in the end.

But things aren't so beautiful right now. Christ fulfilled God's Old Testament promises but then he left—and there are the deceiving beauties, and there is waiting. So much waiting.

We are confounded and even despairing, trying to remember what Jesus said, trying to believe that he really did come out of the grave, trying to hold out hope that complete healing is on the horizon.

How do we, then, live in the present, in this already-not-yet? We live as promise-believers in a promise-keeping God. Just as there were promises in the past that God fulfilled, there are promises for the present to which we can cling.

He's proven his heartbeat, the drumbeat of time, in past passionate pursuit:

But God, being rich in mercy, because of the great love with which he loved us, even when we were dead in our trespasses, made us alive together with Christ—by grace you have been saved—and raised us up with him and seated us with him in the heavenly places in Christ Jesus. (Eph. 2:4–6)

He's promised blessing in the future:

So that in the coming ages he might show the immeasurable riches of his grace in kindness toward us in Christ Jesus. For by grace you have been saved through faith. And this is not your own doing; it is the gift of God. (vv. 7–8)

If God has brought beauty (and he has) and is bringing beauty (and he is), then this is how we live in the present:

For we are his workmanship, created in Christ Jesus for good works, which God prepared beforehand, that we should walk in them. (v. 10)

We go all-in on the promise by submitting ourselves to the great Artist as the medium so he might continue communicating to and through us.

God implanted a seed of eternity in our hearts so that we would seek and know that there is more to life than what we can see. There is a place for us that we can't see, pulsating with a heartbeat like a mother's womb. We must start with this very real end in mind and work backward so that we might rest and wait in this wintery world. If God is going to make all things beautiful—every broken heart, every broken relationship, every broken person—we can live another day. We can have hope.

I go to a friend's wedding in a home overlooking the mountains. It's February; snow will come later that night, the trees are bare, and the grass is brittle and yellow. I watch my friend exchange vows and rings and I think of his story. I think of his sobs, his joy lost in an unwanted divorce. I think of his faithfulness in the face of faithlessness, his trust in his God. The officiant pronounces them husband and wife, and my friend's brother, sitting beside me, begins to sob. "It's all over," he whispers. "It's all over." It feels like a finish line of sorts, and we've all crossed over together, fully aware of what it has taken to get here. Knowing the pain and also knowing God's faithfulness makes this moment so very beautiful.

This is the paradox once again. When Jesus's heart started beating again after three days of silence, all those who have ever looked to him as the Seed-Son instantaneously entered God's love and were made right, but we live in this in-between when we can't see this reality with our eyes. We live by faith with a living hope that one day we'll cross a finish line and say, "It's all over."

And then we'll say, through our sobs, "Isn't it beautiful?"

Perpetual Advent

The angels announced his heartbeat. Women ran to tell. The Holy Spirit fell.

We often look back at this moment as the end of the story, but it was really the beginning of the time for healing.

This new era became pregnant again, this time with another promise: the promise of a future grace, a future beauty, and a future home.

What was it he'd said?

I will come again and receive you to Myself.[5]

God is a promising God; we are a people waiting.

The world has filled up again with darkness. Violence, plundering, strife, and iniquity prevail. Perverse judgment proceeds. People are suffering.

How long, O Lord?

I am going to do something in your days that you would not believe, even if I told you.

Never still, God is bringing forth the fullness of time, when time will give way to eternity. Until then, we must wait in perpetual Advent, with eyes open to see and ears cocked to hear.

In what area of your life are you struggling to wait for the fulfilled promise? It is in that very circumstance that God leans down and whispers to you, *I am at work in a way you would not believe if it were told to you.*

The labor pains are increasing, reminding us of his whispered promise: "Surely I am coming quickly" (Rev. 22:20 NKJV).

God kept his first promise to send the Seed, and he will certainly keep the second.

In the meantime, we are his workmanship.

The waiting people, whispering the promise while we wait, say, "Even so, come, Lord Jesus!"

PART THREE

WINTER

Workman: A skilled and artful maker

Workmanship (Greek: *poiema*): something that is composed, constructed, made, or manufactured; a product or design produced by an artisan. *Poiema* means any work of art, such as a statue, a song, architecture, a poem, or a painting. It conveys the idea of something artfully created.

God Is a Potter

He Molds Beauty When We Surrender Control

> For everything there is a season, and a time for
> every matter under heaven: *a time to break down,*
> *and a time to build up.*

J ESUS TEMPORARILY LEFT US in a world full of trouble.
Creation continues in perpetual, groaning labor, and we
feel those pains every day.

I rise in the morning to make breakfast for my insatiable
boys and I drive carpool in the afternoon. In between I string
words on a page, sit across coffee shop tables from women
who face the inconsolable, and work through my own worries
and fears regarding my future and, predominantly, my children's futures. I cannot see the future through the fog, I cannot control or fix or design, and I cannot find the guarantees

to pass out to myself and others that all will turn out as we hope in one year or in twenty.

Sometimes the monotony gets to me and I want to escape, to be free of laundry and lunches, to rest my weary bones from the gnawing imperfections of life.

Sometimes it's ministry life that wearies me. The demands on my time and energy and soul feel too much, the silent hurts too deep, my inadequacies scream too loud, and I want to give up, leaving it all to someone else more qualified, more enthusiastic, less run-down.

Other times I feel the chronic effects of sin, the grief of life's impermanence, or the limits of my own aging body. The news shouts at me incessantly, and I feel helpless to bring about change in the world, much less in my own home.

When I lay my head on the pillow at night, these are the things I think about—my own inconsolable things.

My pastor-husband, too, could tell stories, stories that you're probably already acquainted with because they are yours, ours: adultery, abuse, violation, depression, anger, racism, self-abuse, addiction, lust, abortion, anxiety, divorce, rejection.

A world of trouble it is, and, living in it, we rehearse our persistent internal questions.

Where is the relief? Where was God and where is he now? Where is our help and consolation?

We hold our inconsolable things close, hoping no one will sniff them out. If we do speak of them we do so in private, with hushed tones and many tears, because we feel ashamed that we can't get it together and, truth be told, because we don't want the Band-Aids others might offer, the reciting of Romans 8:28 or Jeremiah 29:11.

Our carefully constructed worldviews are often houses made of cards that can't bear the weight of the inconsolable things. We are the crowd forming around Jesus, waving our expectations with the palm branches: *we will worship you if you let us mold you.*

The original crucifixion crowd twisted his words in order to make them fit what they wanted. We do the same. And what do we want? Immediate fixes, perfection in an imperfect world. We work hard to ignore what Jesus said about trouble in this world, about always having the poor with us, about how his friends will share in his sufferings, about pointing to a disabled man as the means to display God's work.

Our ears are tickled everywhere we turn these days. We're sold a bill of goods that offers what Jesus did not say in place of what he did. We pursue the false comfort of "now," the empty promises of "instant," and the urge to "dream" of what could be—in Jesus's name, of course. We're told that becoming a Christian should make our lives easier, better. There is a market available for us when we wrap our ambitions and desires for self-glory in Christian terms. Displacing the whole counsel of God, we instead search for Instagram mantras that make us feel better for a moment. We go to churches that offer pep and happy and three steps to a better life without ever addressing the inconsolable things hanging over every heart in the room. When it happens to us—when we're the heavy heart in the room—we hide behind a smile, as has been modeled for us. Sweep all the inconsolable things away into the corner where we can pretend they're not there. Make believe Scripture doesn't say, "There is a time for weeping and mourning," and give no space to those among us who actually are at this very moment weeping and mourning.

We don't often speak of suffering, of sacrifice, of self-denial, of death, of embracing all that God gives, no matter what it is, so that he might receive glory. We prefer to believe he's there to make us, ultimately, what we want to be. *We prefer a God we can mold.*

While we lap up this bill of goods, we wonder where Jesus is and why he's not moving according to our Instagram mantras. Why does suffering continue to cling to us as if it's a member of the family? We must be doing something to make God angry! (This is what we say to ourselves.) Why do we have these ongoing unmet desires? We must not have enough faith! Why can't we shake this sense of longing? We must not be working hard enough!

No. It is simply that we haven't listened to Jesus. The Word has said it all along: we are meant to live with imperfections and things left undone in the present. Jesus doesn't give us our dreams and stuff himself inside our stories; we are for his dream and his story. He is the workman, and we are the workmanship.

We cannot bear this thought. *I* cannot bear this thought. I adore and embrace the privileges of following after Christ, but I don't much care for the call to submission and the lack of control. I don't much care for the paradoxical nature of the kingdom he rules, and, in fact, as I've established, I prefer to ignore the paradox completely. When trouble comes or when I can't for the life of me get the inconsolable things fixed, I'm astonished, surprised, and quick to point an accusatory finger toward God. I close my ears and hum in solidarity with my brothers and sisters in the crowd who want to mold him to reflect their own desires.

Only One Hero

I go to a nice hotel in a cosmopolitan city, free to myself for a night, an introvert mother's dream. The room is perfection, the bed fluffy and piled high with comfortable pillows. It's as if I am the first one to stay in this room; it's mine, it belongs to me alone. A luxurious picture of cleanliness, quiet, everything in its place. I wake in the morning, traipse to the shower—and there find an unfamiliar hair in the tub circling around the drain and I'm suddenly considering all of the many people who have slept in "my" bed and showered in "my" tub. Perhaps even the night before I'd arrived, a perfect stranger was here, in this room, luxuriating in my hotel room, feeling like a king or queen. Where I had the night before been the center of the universe, I am now reminded, in one long brown strand of hair, that I'm most assuredly not and that soon someone will come after me. There is a bigger story playing out, each hotel room renter a bit part. The world, in fact, doesn't revolve around me or bend to my wishes; I'm not the hero of this story.

This is our problem in the present waiting: we all want to be the hero of the story and we're waiting for our story to finally begin, to finally take off. In our stories, we the heroes are forever capable of overcoming suffering to win the day, the girl (or the boy), and the glory.

When we, trying to assert ourselves as the hero in the paradox kingdom, find ourselves unable to win the day, much less the glory, we are flummoxed and then driven toward despair and on further into depression, or we're driven to anger and on further to pride and paranoia.

Woes upon woes to the hero-wannabe, because there is only room for One. When we try to take up his mantle, we fruitlessly strive as if the clay were forcefully resisting the potter's hands:

> Woe to him who strives with him who formed him, a
>   pot among earthen pots!
> Does the clay say to him who forms it, "What are
>   you making?"
> or "Your work has no handles"?
> Woe to him who says to a father, "What are you
>   begetting?"
> or to a woman, "With what are you in labor?"
>   (Isa. 45:9–10)

God, the potter, speaks to the clay—his people who are suffering (and questioning) his workmanship:

> Thus says the LORD,
>   the Holy One of Israel, and the one who formed
>   him:
> "Ask me of things to come;
>   will you command me concerning my children
>   and the work of my hands?
> I made the earth
>   and created man on it;
> it was my hands that stretched out the heavens,
>   and I commanded all their host." (vv. 11–12)

When God spoke those words, he already had plans in mind of using a heathen king to do his bidding so that his children, who were suffering in their present state, would be brought together again and restored to beauty.

In other words, there is only one Hero in the kingdom of God, and he will do whatever it takes to make all things beautiful, even if it must come through exile and suffering. These are painful, awful things, as are our various present trials to us, and no one is denying that, least of all our God. But the promise always remains: a Hero who gets the girl and, with his love, makes her beautiful.

We don't wonder if God can make good out of bad; we just don't like that it comes that way. We are the clay telling the potter how to mold us. We crave hero-glory for ourselves, not for the true Hero.

We don't want a God we can't command.

The Pattern of Providence

> A time to be born, a time to die;
> a time to plant, and a time to pluck up what is
> planted. . . .
> For everything there is a season, and a time for every
> matter under heaven. (Eccles. 3:2,1)

A season, a specific time, for everything. And all of the specifics of our seasons are determined by God.

Although God has put eternity in our hearts, he has also made us limited. We are people of a season, a time, seeing only what is present and in front of us. We're unable to figure God out from alpha to omega; we're also unable to figure out the pattern of our lives or of this world from beginning to end.

Again, we fight. We don't want a God we can't command, but we also don't want a God we can't decipher. If we're honest, it's more the *plan* of God for which we'd like to have the secret code. God can remain mysterious just as long as we are given his plan in step-by-step order. *Then* we could really get behind this God, *then* we could really walk by faith, *then* we could live as overcomers while we wait for all things to be made beautiful.

We plead, we cajole; we figure and analyze, plan and control. We simply cannot embrace the complexities and mysteries of life, even though it's spoken in clear language in the Scriptures that "he has put eternity into man's heart, *yet so that he cannot find out what God has done from the beginning to the end*" (Eccles. 3:11, emphasis added). And what comes just before these words? "He has made everything beautiful in its time."

These two truths provide a lifetime of tension: God makes all things beautiful, yet we can't know exactly how. We may never know.

Everyone wants to "find out" and understand the ways of God and just how, exactly, he is making things culminate in beauty, but none can. The word translated "find," or "find out," has the sense of "figure out." The preacher who wrote these words thus realized that both his desire to understand all of life, as well as the limitations on his ability to do so, were ordained by God.[1]

Those who've come before us, from Abraham to Augustine, couldn't figure it out. They were limited by era and age, just as we are. We can know *God* but we cannot know *his plans* in full. We're limited by seasons and cycles. As Matthew Henry says, "We . . . must not expect to find the world more sure to us than it has been to others."[2]

This is meant to be encouraging. It's as if God is allowing us a rest while he does the heavy lifting. We don't have to navigate or figure; we don't have to calculate. He expects that we'll trust his heart and intentions and lie down as clay on the potter's wheel. It seems as if this posture of trust and submission is the only way we can rest, really rest, with inconsolable things roiling in our hearts.

He's given us reasons to trust, for hope always has its reasons.

We can first hang our hope on the unfolding narrative of redemption in Scripture. So again, we look back at how God has acted in the past so we can recognize him in our present.

Even in the earliest of days, there were people holding inconsolable things. And God was there, seeing and sculpting in patient providence.

First on record was Job, the man we admire but hope never to become. Satan had a go at him, taking everything but his life. His friends, at first extending grace with their silence, began speaking the bill of goods: the innocent prosper (and therefore you must have sinned to deserve this); the truly repentant would not suffer so (and therefore you must have some repenting to do); the one who fears God is protected from disaster (and therefore you must not have enough faith); the wicked are the ones who are punished like this (and therefore you must be counted among them).

Job carried on, weeping and mourning, and rightly so. But he also wanted answers, and when God finally appeared to speak with him, God didn't reprimand his grief; he reprimanded Job's demands and hopelessness. In other words, Job clearly wanted to figure out the plan from beginning to end, to understand why and what and how. God, not giving a why or what or how, only called to mind the complexity and beauty of life and asked Job not to forget his hope—that the God who created beauty and joy and all good things could possibly restore to him something beautiful and joyful and good. He pointed to the unseen beginning of time, the unknowable number of stars, the indiscoverable depths of the sea, and the invisible storehouses of snow as evidence not only of undeniable created beauty but a design and plan known only to God. God played the Creator card as well as the Providence card.

Job, reminded of whom the Hero truly is, humbly responded:

> I know that you can do all things,
>   and that no purpose of yours can be thwarted. . . .
> Therefore I have uttered what I did not understand,
>   things too wonderful for me, which I did not
>   know. . . .
> I had heard of you by the hearing of the ear,
>   but now my eye sees you;
> therefore I despise myself,
>   and repent in dust and ashes. (Job 42:2–6)

I imagine Job's tears and grief remained, but in this moment he became supple, moldable clay in the loving hands of his Potter.

Moving along the timeline of redemptive history, we find Naomi, an embittered Hebrew woman who lost her husband, her children, her prosperity, and her hope for a bright future. In a melodramatic moment, she renames herself Mara, meaning "bitter." She returns, pitiful and poor, to her homeland with a foreign daughter-in-law, Ruth, whom she relies on to gather their food from what is left by harvesters in the field. On Naomi's part, there is a sense of sulking and depression and profound hopelessness. Unlike with Job, God doesn't speak to Naomi. Instead he orchestrates, beginning even with the harvest they've returned to, providential planning at its best. And then Ruth "happens" to glean in the fields of Boaz, a distant relative. We could go back even further to see how God prepared for Ruth and Naomi: a statute in his law, written generations before, commanding harvesters to provide for the poor by letting them follow behind and glean. Another statute, written perhaps just for this very moment, providing for widows through a kinsman-redeemer. God's hand is in it all, preparing the scene far in advance. Through all of these things, God arranges a marriage for Ruth and Boaz and gives Naomi a grandson. She'd returned to Bethlehem empty but becomes profoundly full.

These are but two stories within the larger grand arc of Scripture, but in them we see a pattern, a blueprint drawn and executed by Patient Providence. We cannot command this Providence and we cannot figure out his ways from beginning to end, but we can trust his heart and intentions. Even in the midst of horrendous suffering, God never leaves, never shames, and never is sidetracked from his goal of bringing redemptive beauty.

Wrestle or Rest

What does this say to us in our present day? How do our stories fit in the larger arc of his story?

At a point when I faced profound suffering as a young mother, I remember sitting at a traffic light with tears running down my face, my precious boy in the backseat. A difficult diagnosis had come a few days prior, and all I wanted to do was rewind time, to unhear the words that had upended my world.

I considered how I'd seen others endure challenges and suffering and I immediately thought of a friend who had a

child with severe disabilities and how lovingly and intention-
ally she parented him. And then I remembered how she'd said
that, through this child, she'd had countless opportunities to
spread God's fame. She, as I, was in a position of influence
in our church, so many people saw how she handled herself
and many heard her words about her child and about God.

As I. The thought struck me that I, too, had this opportunity—
to be the example, to be the tangible display of God's glory.
And, like a toddler, I wanted to turn away from God with
folded arms and pouting lips.

I don't want to be the example.

It was an everyday moment—turning my car right on red—
and all of my thought processes happened in a flash, but it
was a moment of clarity. I knew I had a choice. I could keep
my crossed arms and closed fists firmly in place and seek
solace in food or sleep or my own bitterness, or I could lift
my hands in surrender to Providence and walk expectantly
down the road he'd mapped out for me, searching for his
beauty in my suffering.

Nothing changed in that moment—not my circumstances,
my pain, my grief, my desperation, nothing.

Nothing changed except the posture of my heart.

What happened for Job and for Naomi is the same thing
that happened for me: God was asking to break me down
in order for his name to be built up, not in some narcissistic
way but in a clay-and-potter sort of way. He was asking me
to submit to the unchangeable blueprints in a way that would
build beauty rather than bitterness, faith rather than futility,
for his glory and for my good.

There is beauty, I have since discovered, even in the breaking down, in the process of becoming, in the humbling and

the submitting to Patient Providence. We must not forget the paradox kingdom Jesus instituted in which the broken down are lifted up, the humble celebrated and exalted. As we break ourselves down in submission, he is built up in our minds, hearts, and lives, and we actually experience a kind of freedom found in no other way. In releasing our control, beauty finds us, because in our helplessness and surrender, we find that God walks near to us.

As we humble ourselves, we're no longer blinded by self but are able to see God at work in the present. We're the moldable clay on the potter's wheel, in process of becoming a piece of art, feeling and responding to even the slightest movement and noticing God everywhere.

If Naomi had not renamed herself Mara and wallowed in her bitterness, she might have noticed God's presence and help: Ruth's constant companionship, the renewal and rebirth of her homeland, and the wink-wink coincidence of Ruth finding herself on Boaz's property.

As I myself relaxed into God the Potter's hands, I began noticing and even celebrating his slightest movements: a word of encouragement spoken, a hand of help in a difficult moment, a person expertly placed in my life. Patient Providence had been planning and preparing for my suffering all along. My circumstances didn't and won't ever change in this life, but it's a beautiful thing to be free from trying to control them in order to avoid pain, to be free from the power of fear concerning the future and of death, to be at rest by faith in the hands of Patient Providence. I'm certainly not perfect in this—this also is an inconsolable thing—but there is nothing more beautiful for me than when my soul is at rest, even in imperfection.

The blueprint has not changed from Job's day, nor Naomi's, nor the day when Jesus was murdered: he will make his beauty in his way in his people in his time.

While the clay cannot mold the potter, we can and must mold and shape our hearts to fit the potter's design. This is the ongoing work of the Christian, to say without equivocation, "As the clay, I am the thing being shaped, and I certainly don't know more than the providential Potter."

We are all the young mother at the stoplight faced with a choice: wrestle or rest. Certainly, we must wrestle our hearts into rest, but in continually wrestling without finally resting—and God will give you this option, waiting patiently by—we will ask why for our entire lives. In resting, we don't escape suffering, grief, or inconsolable things but we stand in a hope that a greater story is unfolding and, in seeing the story arc, we're able to see our own lives in sharper focus, through a lens of beauty.

Are you in turmoil right now? Are you the one sitting at the stoplight with a choice before you? This is what I would say to you: God is up to something. Break yourself down before him, submit to his indecipherable plan, and watch eagerly for the beauty to come. As Matthew Henry wrote:

> Every thing is as God has made it; it is really as he appointed it to be, not as it appears to us. That which to us seems most unpleasant is yet, in its proper time, altogether becoming. Cold is becoming in winter as heat in summer; and the night, in its turn, is a black beauty, as the day, in its turn, is a bright one.[3]

Climb onto the Potter's wheel and rest from your wrestling.

God Is a Composer

He Leads and Helps
As We Tune Ourselves to His Spirit

For everything there is a season, and a time for
every matter under heaven: *a time to weep, and
a time to laugh; a time to mourn, and a time to
dance.*

WHEN WE LIE IN REST, prone beneath the Potter's
hands, the twisting and turning of the wheel may
often feel disorienting. We've given ourselves over to Another,
and we can't see what we'll eventually be or how, as a vessel,
we might be used, nor can we imagine how our suffering may
be transformed into beauty. Trusting an unseen and unexpected God with our most vulnerable cares can feel risky,

because we're spinning out of our own control. We may feel we've been left to ourselves, left to our own devices, left to decipher how to live well in this in-between.

The truth is that we *are* out of our own control—but we aren't left alone. We spin beneath loving hands that are in control of all things.

And it turns out we are being molded into vessels made specifically for filling. The Potter sings himself into the clay, into us. We have this treasure in our jars of clay: he has poured himself into our hearts.

He has given us his Holy Spirit.

The Helper

The word used to describe the Holy Spirit in Scripture is *Paraclete*, which some translate "Comforter." Although he certainly consoles us in our grief, the more precise meaning is "with strength." R. C. Sproul says, "The Holy Spirit . . . comes to the people of Christ not to heal their wounds after a battle but to strengthen them before and during a struggle."[1]

To those who bemoaned Jesus's departure, he comforted them in the face of their unremoved inconsolable things, saying, "It is better that I go away."[2] What could be better than Jesus among us, calming our storms, healing our sick, raising our dead, and turning our everyday drinking water into wine? We'd rather have sight than faith, skin than Spirit.

However, Jesus said it is better for us to have the Holy Spirit, because he is not just God dwelling with us; he is God dwelling *within* us. Faith and the Spirit and future permanent healing are apparently of greater value in this kingdom of his than sight and skin, instant and tangible, painless and instantly perfected.

In fact, when the disciples reveled in the presence of the risen Christ, they asked him, "'Lord, will you at this time restore the kingdom to Israel?' He said to them, 'It is not for you to know times or seasons that the Father has fixed by his own authority. But you will receive power when the Holy Spirit has come upon you'" (Acts 1:6–8).

Jesus alluded to the mystery of life, their unfulfilled longings for justice and beauty. He turned their attention away from trying to calculate the hand of God and discern the future by saying, "You have the Holy Spirit."

And he is enough.

He is enough because he is present in our present, a constant companion. He is enough because he mourns with us over the sin done to us and grieves over our own sin, yet constantly invites us to experience forgiveness and pass it out generously to others. He is enough because, by confirming to us that we're secure in the Everlasting Arms, he helps us laugh at the future. He is enough because we never weep alone and our hearts, even in the face of pain, know a hope and a joy that make them dance as we grieve.

He is not simply enough. The Holy Spirit is a beautiful life song—he is abundant, he is our sufficiency for ministry, he enables us with his strength and power to face the day, and he is jealously persistent for our good.

God's plan is not to fix the temporarily unfixable, no matter how much we think it should be. He's not going to show us the future or give us a formula that will allow us to gain control of our lives, because he will not allow us to live independent of his Spirit. He wants us to see beauty in the face of pain, and we cannot see it without him.

He's not going to give us independence, because he's given us his Spirit-song, breathing himself into our souls. When we know love as his heart's intention, his song becomes our own, spilling over the sides of our jars of clay.

In fact, our weak and breakable jars point to the treasure of Christ and his gospel: we endure pain, mirroring what he endured unto death, but our pain is different precisely *because* of the pain he endured. Not only are we *not* fully crushed by our pain but our pain can be resurrected into beauty *because* Christ's death turned into life. For those who look to Christ by faith, his resurrected life fills us with himself and then flows out of us to display his power, even and especially in our inconsolable things.

Master Composer

God is called Skilled Creator; he is called Potter; he is said to be the Refiner who, like a goldsmith, uses fire. And he is also called Poet. God in Us, the Holy Spirit, desires to compose a poem with our lives. He is a lyricist, carving us with words; a singer giving us a song; an author setting the rhyme and rhythm of our lives. This is the beautiful work of the Holy Spirit, who undergirds us with the truth of Christ, convicts us of sin, transforms us into Christ-likeness, and causes us to explode with works and words of worship.

This is what I wish I could understand fully: that he is the Poet, the Master Composer, not I. My human heart can only formulate standards I myself must keep in order to please him, to earn his audience. *I* determine what I must do. *I* measure if I'm succeeding or failing. *I* must author a story with my life that is honorable and filled with good deeds that will change the world. *I* must console myself or lead myself through the valley of the shadow of death.

No, no, no. Jesus said that, because of what he did, not only is my sin erased—no self-made formula needed—but I've also been given all the riches of his righteousness simply out of God's kindness. *He* is my leader now; *he* is the author and perfecter of my faith. In following him, walking in step with the Spirit, I can't miss the song he's writing with me; in fact, his leading itself is like a poetic song I can't get out of my head or my heart.

As the song being written by a Master Composer, I must follow. I must tune my instrument to him and respond according to his lead.

Songs of Joy and Freedom

I go to a children's concert as a chaperone with my son's class. On stage sit three men—a cellist, a violinist, and a pianist—and as they begin to play, the auditorium, full of wriggling grade-school students, magically grows still, all ears collectively straining to hear each instrument's sound.

Before the concert, we were told to listen for the emotions expressed in the music. I attempt to listen through the children's ears, wondering what they hear and how they'd describe the notes fluttering and falling all around them. I wonder if they are aware of the value of this performance, of the classical works they're hearing, or the lifelong, tireless practice that's made the performance possible.

I mostly stare at the pianist's hands as they move up and down the keys. I'm a pianist myself, certainly not a professional, but I took piano lessons until I was eighteen. I hated every theory test, scale lesson, and piano contest until my mom allowed me to quit, and only then did I discover music could come from a place of joy and expression rather than simply obligation or pushing keys in the way the sheet music instructed. When I discovered what it was to express a song and move along at the impulse of the composer who wrote each piece I played, I found the beauty of music.

This is the way of the Spirit as well. Christ has fulfilled the law for us; because of him, we are safe and secure in the love of the Father. The Spirit seals us with this love as a guarantee and continually brings this truth to mind, setting a song of joy in our hearts and conducting us to play our notes as he leads.

We have died and been broken by the law but built up and made whole by the Spirit, and now we're able to be filled by his power and able to be used by him as well. He takes our submission to him and fills us with his song so others might hear and know his love for themselves.

There is present beauty in knowing our present God and playing our instrument in response to his lead.

I look over at a teacher who I know plays the violin and wonder if she's thinking the same sorts of things, paying close attention to the violinist's bow and drawing inspiration for the next time she picks up her own. Perhaps, as I am in that moment, she is plotting how to incorporate the beauty of music into her life even more. Different instruments, same song.

I wonder if the children hear. Most of them look bored; some occupy themselves by clapping along to a staccato song but quickly move off beat and disrupt the concert. They cannot know, because they are only children, but they are experiencing a moment of unadulterated beauty. Bach and Gershwin are visiting us through time, and all of this is a giant pointer finger toward God.

I wish we all understood this, especially the Christians, especially *me*. In the past, Jesus died and rose again. In the future, we'll have him in all his perfect beauty. Now, in the present, the Holy Spirit is the primary worker, singing a siren song to the Truth seeker and composing in us beauty from pain and life from death. He is helping us understand Jesus and how Jesus reversed the curse on our behalf.

I close my eyes and listen to the concert. I can't see the composer but I hear his song and see the effects of his composition all around.

Understanding this truth makes all the difference, and it's what I think of as I sit and listen to the music in the school auditorium. It stirs me not because I'm a pianist or because the songs are professionally played but because I imagine myself as the piano keys, as God's instrument, playing according to the lead of the Master Composer. Only when I'm looking for his lead *and trusting that he will lead in a way I can't miss* am I able to know the joy of closing my eyes, feeling the music pulse through me, and knowing how very good God is. This joy of his—that he presses into me—is my strength.

I'm not meant to live in honor of him while apart from him, as if he's the critic in the audience. I'm meant to live in honor of him by abiding in him and believing the Composer-Poet will help me express his song through my instrument. This is freedom!

This is no dead composer. He is living and active, even in the midst of my inconsolable things. Praise him that we're left in inconsolable things but we are not left without God!

See, this is the crux of it all, that we have a God who is all-powerful, all-knowing, and all-good, all at the same time. According to Jonathan Edwards, because God holds all power and wisdom and goodness, we can find comfort when we question his providence and our circumstances.[3] Just think of a different combination—any different combination. All-powerful without being all-good. All-good without being all-knowing. All-knowing without being all-powerful. He is the perfect Composer; we can trust his pressing as we lay prone as his keyboard.

Rather than becoming embittered by what God has not granted us (namely, the ability to comprehend all of reality), we should enjoy the gifts that God *has* given.[4] He gives himself: his presence rather than his plan, his providence rather than his plan, his power rather than his plan, his promises rather than his plan. We can seek God and cling to him and leave it to him to make sense of it all; we have to trust he's composing a beautiful song-poem with our lives, which we exhibit by keeping in step with the Spirit.

But just how do we do that? How do we tune ourselves to him?

Move by the Spirit

Galatians 5 says that we're to respond to the Holy Spirit in various modes of movement: we're to "walk by the Spirit," be "led by the Spirit," and "keep in step with the Spirit." Paul's words make me think of a child trying to match their parent's steps; there is a very real sense of who is leading and who is following. Our role is the child's: we're to consistently follow the leading of the Holy Spirit, trusting fully that he will always lead us to righteousness and into the truth and life of Jesus Christ.

But how do we know his leading?

I've had the impression at times that walking by the Spirit should be an emotional experience or feel as if I've somehow been transported supernaturally to a state of euphoria. I've complicated the matter further by assuming there should be tangible evidence of his presence and leadership in my life, which usually means I want him to move or provide on my terms.

Although difficult to fully understand, moving by the Spirit and staying in step with him is a manner of life that is dominated, controlled, and influenced by him. It is to live in a constant and consistent attitude of submission to the Spirit, whose role in our lives, among other things, is to teach us, guide us into all truth, convict us of sin, and put to death the deeds of the body.

This happens through the moment-to-moment yielding to his prompting. This may be a tug on our conscience or a check in our spirit or a thought in our heads. We need to be sensitive to these sometimes very brief moments and consider if the Spirit is pressing on us.[5]

Many times in Scripture, when the Holy Spirit leads people, they have a sense of being sent out, to "go." "Go" is a huge clue to us that the Holy Spirit is leading, because go seems to be his favorite word. Jesus said the Holy Spirit's role would be to bring to remembrance all of what he said while he was on earth. What did he say in regard to the Holy Spirit?

"Go therefore and make disciples . . . and lo, I am with you always, even to the end of the age" (Matt. 28:19–20 NKJV).

And again in Acts 1:8, "You will receive power when the Holy Spirit has come upon you, and you will be my witnesses."

We will go and be his witnesses, and the One who will lead us to do this is the Spirit. That's what Jesus said. So when you hear a persistent "go," whether it's to go across the street or across the world, it's likely the Holy Spirit.

In addition, Jesus said we'd be strengthened to go by the Holy Spirit. If *go* is the Holy Spirit's favorite word, helping is his favorite action. *Go and I will help you.*

Follow the leader.

Besides waiting for a "go," we can and we must cultivate staying in step with the Spirit in our lives. That begins with the transforming of our minds, which is accomplished through diligent, prayerful, and submissive study of the Word of God.

In John 16:13, Jesus tells us, "when the Spirit of truth comes, he will guide you into all the truth." A chapter later, he clarifies where truth is found: "Sanctify them by Your truth. Your word is truth" (17:17 NKJV).

Setting our minds on the Spirit is not clearing our minds; it is filling our minds with the Word of God. We will more clearly know his prompting when we know the Scripture.

The Minor Key of Conviction

The pianist grabs a microphone and asks the children, who are getting restless and wiggly, for their help in choosing the final piece. Do they prefer slow and quiet or fast and loud?

The entire audience screams at once: "Fast!" He smiles know-ingly. The children clap their hands in anticipation as the cellist and violinist perch their bows. And then they are off, the pianist streaming his hands up and down the keys, the room pulsating with energy. The music makes me think of a galloping horse or a grasshopper jumping on hot cement. The musicians bob their heads and smile as the children begin to clap along; I wonder if they've even prepared a slow song at all. Perhaps they do this at every concert—offering a choice but already knowing what the final answer will be.

We all choose the upbeat music, the kind you can clap along with, those songs that remind us of happy things, dancing and laughing. The happy songs are typically stacked with major chords, which were my first lessons in piano: C, E, and G. (I can hear the chord in my head as I pretend-play it on my writing desk.) I much preferred when my piano teacher gave me sheet music written in major keys, because then I didn't have to concentrate on remembering which notes were flat or sharp and I could breeze through the piece. The minor keys were much more difficult to play and, anyway, they made the piece sound forlorn and depressing. If the piece switched keys from major to minor and back to major again, I remember feeling a sense of relief and even audibly sighing when I was able to return "home" to the major key and bring the piece to its conclusion. Happy again.

We choose major keys, but sometimes the Composer, from a place of love, chooses the minor, the kind reminiscent of weeping and mourning. Although we don't necessarily like them, we need the minor keys just as much as the major. Sometimes he wants to convey a truth that is best expressed in a minor key. We cannot know the reasons from beginning to end, but one thing we must know: the piece *will* turn again to the major chords. Weeping will turn to laughing, mourning will again turn to dancing. In the middle, when the key calls for minor, we must not fear. The Spirit is there, composing with minor notes. We must simply walk forward in step with him, trusting. When he pushes on us like piano keys, we obey, we acquiesce. We emit a mournful sound, but we do so with faith of what is to come, knowing even then there is a uniquely beautiful sound of faith in the minor key.

The minor key the Holy Spirit most often wants to play in us is the deep weight of conviction, which leads us into and through the process of repentance and restoration. I know it's his conviction when, through Scripture or through a faithful brother or sister, he points to a specific sin in my life and then offers me forgiveness and help in order to change. His conviction is both pointed and hopeful. It may be the Holy Spirit leading us to do something that our common sense or logic resists, such as forgiving a betrayal or loving our neighbor as we would ourselves. The discomfort we feel in conviction is the crucifixion of our flesh: God wants us resting in the finished work of Christ rather than seeking validation and approval from others; he wants us listening and waiting, poised to obey where he leads, rather than listening to the insistent and persistent scream of our flesh to do great works in order to prove ourselves worthy and admirable. We recognize this tendency only when God's hands press on the minor keys. We need to mourn our insufficiency in order to dance again in the sufficiency of Christ.

Last week, the mourning for me was small, some sort of sickness that sent me to bed for several days. When I am still and unproductive, the voice of my flesh always begins screaming. A battle rages inside—the battle that comes when I'm unable to do much of anything; when I'm unable to prove my value, earn my keep; when I'm isolated from people and unable to keep the world spinning around, as I tend to believe that I do. To me, work equals earned love and performance equals proven value. My striving, I too often believe, justifies me in the sight of people and, probably more so, in the sight of myself.

I know this is my flesh screaming, but it screams so loud and so persistently that I am deeply uncomfortable as I try to shush it. It screams at me about my own cracks, telling me to rise up and do something about them. I know it's not truth because, according to Truth, I am justified forever. In him, I am secure in love. So why do I fear? My underlying fear is that I will disappoint, be criticized, be found lacking. I imagine they—whoever "they" might be—are whispering constantly of my lack, of my faults, of what I should be doing but am not. "Who does she think she is?" That's what the voices say. My fear of other people and the flesh's compulsion to please them loom larger than my awe of God.

The Spirit-song has been muted by desires for self-glory.

It would feel to me like moving from a minor to major key if I simply gave in to my flesh, started a list of good works, and attacked them one by one for all those demanding, inquiring minds to see. I'd be able to quiet the restlessness and reassure myself, albeit with false comfort.

Of course, none of this is conscious thinking, until the Holy Spirit presses a mournful key—a song to humble myself, confess, and repent. I must sit in the discomfort that it is to my flesh of walking in step with the Spirit, for the flesh fights against the Spirit and the Spirit against the flesh. I must allow

God to crucify my flesh, inflamed with its need for approval and validation, and rest in the completed work of Jesus.

Whatever your natural compulsions are, the Holy Spirit will pursue you with conviction. We must stay in the minor key as long as he has us there, because the Holy Spirit's conviction and kindness drawing us to repentance is evidence of his love, and repentance turns the music to a major key once again.

The Major Key of Composition

Amazingly, God not only takes our pain and gives us a song but also gives us a song to sing over the pain and needs of others. We're given, in other words, not just the presence of Christ in the Holy Spirit but also the *power* of Christ in the Holy Spirit in order to stand in our inconsolable things and to minister to others in theirs. As we let his song spill forth out of us, we are an integral part of God making all things beautiful in this world.

Paul says it like this: "For we are his workmanship, created in Christ Jesus for good works, which God prepared beforehand, that we should walk in them" (Eph. 2:10).

Jesus in us—the Holy Spirit—is at this very moment composing us for his glory and for the benefit of others. He is empowering us through the unique gifts and abilities he's given us to communicate about himself through our lives.

Different instruments, same song.

He also—and this is very important—authors the use of those gifts. My fear is that we don't hear the Spirit song moving us to dance or weep or sing because we're more interested in self-glory or self-composition. Nothing causes the Spirit more grief than the idolatry of trying to take glory and opportunities for redemption away from God or resisting the twists and turns he wants to take in the music.

We must rest in the authorship of the Holy Spirit and obey his leading, no matter where he wants to take us. So what if the poem doesn't rhyme? So what if the song is written in a minor key? God has already prepared how he will make a beautiful work out of our lives. We might as well fall back into his arms and feel the song of love he wants to sing over and through us.

We live heavy and sluggish and overwhelmed because we look at the Christian life as if we're keys that need to push ourselves. We believe we're the mathematicians who will fix the inconsolable things. We're quick to run forward like warriors into the world, but unless it's initiated, led, and fueled by the Holy Spirit, we're only left with a restless feeling inside and a constant feeling of hopelessness, because there is always something more we can do.

But when we learn the voice of the Spirit and commit to obeying him, we cannot miss his leading and prompting. We'll find our hands and hearts, as the hymn says,[6] moving at the impulse of his love. His song will become ours. The Spirit-led aren't trying to change the world so much as they are trying to allow God to change them in a way that spills over like a song into the world.

Of course, he will take us in directions we never dreamed or imagined. Walking in step with the Spirit may mean doing something that doesn't make total sense or is different from fellow Christians around us. It may mean saying no or doing something incredibly difficult that can only really be done supernaturally. Yes, it may even mean pain. A Spirit-led person is one who knows that happiness and safety aren't guaranteed in this world. In every way, there is a vulnerability to walking in step with the Spirit, because it's a constant acknowledgment that we're not in charge and that we belong to someone else. However uncomfortable it is, we are waiting for the beautiful moment when the minor key switches to major again.

Supernatural Chords

At the concert, I marveled at the technique and prowess of the players, but the music mostly made me think about the composers. What inspired Bach toward that melody? What was he expressing with the staccato notes and with the somber ones?

On the piano the notes are just notes, just as the words in a poem or the lyrics in a line of music are just words. It's who strings them together and the message behind the words that make them powerful. The sum is greater than the parts. Unexplainable power is infused into a musical selection at the direction and genius of the composer.

I think of the Holy Spirit. We are but keys on an instrument, flat and emitting a singular sound, but somehow the Spirit takes our self-offering and multiplies it, filling us in with others to make chords, making something grander happen than we could ever form on our own. He is able, because he is God, to make something bigger out of us than what we naturally are. He's able to take the events and circumstances of our lives and form a beautiful composition infused with meaning.

I sit and listen to the music and I'm joyful, at peace, laughing at the future.

You, too, are a note in the chord the Holy Spirit is playing. Your broken clay jar, your story of redemption, your skills, your relationships, even your greatest pain—all of these are a part of the song he's composing in and through you. If he calls us through a song we can't get out of our heads, how is he leading you? How is he convicting you? Where would he have you sing his song of love into this world?

When you know the Holy Spirit pulsing through you, you will hear his present song all around, and you will sing and dance along. You will become the very beauty he's creating out of brokenness in this world.

God Is Our Betrothed

He Builds Beauty While We Wait with Faith

For everything there is a season, and a time for
every matter under heaven: *a time to cast away
stones, and a time to gather stones together.*

A S WE HOLD IN OUR HANDS the promise that all will
eventually be made beautiful and look around at this
life, we know something is wrong. Why would God have left us
in this mess, and what do we do in the meantime? The promise
is sometimes difficult to hear, to remember, and above all to
believe. If only Jesus had taken us with him, if only the inconsolable things were immediately consoled, if only we were in the
presence of the Father instead of left with the invisible Spirit.

When the disciple Peter was in the presence of Jesus, he
spoke out loud the longing that's reverberated in hearts for

generations. Like a child clinging to his parent's leg, Peter asked our own pleading question: "Where are you going, Lord?"[1] And suddenly, like a child watching his parent leave, we too cry out in panic, worried that our feeling of home and comfort and security will never return. *Why are you leaving? Take us with you into All Things Beautiful!*

As I reassured my own children when they were small, Jesus reassured Peter. "Where I'm going you can't follow now, but you'll follow me afterward."[2]

Afterward.

Peter couldn't have known in that moment what would come between "now" and "afterward" for him. He'd deny the very One to whom he was clinging. He'd be led as a sheep to slaughter, in imitation of his Christ. Could he even imagine there would be a you or a me, or just how much time Jesus meant by "afterward"?

And yet here we are. The clock of time ticked on past Peter's generation, and this world two thousand years later has seen just about all there is to see. As a race, we're characterized as inventors of evil things and we've pierced ourselves through with our own inventions. We're sick beneath our sin and the sin done against us. We certainly understand Peter's pleading, perhaps more than he himself did. Knowing all we now know, we'd have joined in his desperate chorus, and we do—pleading for mercy, for relief from the groaning, for rescue from the darkness of our own making.

When will the "afterward" finally come? When will this waiting by faith finally break through to seeing and touching and smelling and tasting and hearing that glorious voice welcoming us home?

The Waiting Bride

The answer lies with our Betrothed.

In the ancient days, Jewish engagements were called betrothals, and they resembled our modern marriage covenants more than our modern engagements. When a Jewish man asked a woman's father for her hand, if he agreed, the man and the woman's father together entered into a contract that, if broken, required divorce proceedings. The man and woman did not consummate their contracted marriage until their wedding day, but they were bound together upon their betrothal as if they were already wed. Consider Joseph when he discovered Mary was pregnant. In his mind, she'd broken their marriage contract and, before an angel from God intervened, he planned to divorce her because of her supposed indiscretion.

The betrothal period existed primarily for the groom's preparation for his bride and the bride's for her groom. The groom prepared by constructing a marriage home for himself and his bride, typically a new addition built onto the side of his father's house. With the ink still drying on the marriage contract, the groom would set off for his father's home with a promise to return for the bride when all was ready. No one, including the groom himself, could give a precise date when he'd complete his work and return for her.

The bride's preparation was simply to faithfully wait.

Perhaps each day she recalled her beloved's voice in her head, remembering its lilt, straining to hear him calling in the streets, the announcement that their wedding day had finally arrived. Rachel, we know from Genesis 29, had to wait seven years for her groom, Jacob, and then another seven days when her father deceived him using Leah. Jacob loved Rachel and certainly Rachel anticipated a happy union, so her wait must've felt like thousands of years. But it's all she, or any bride for that matter, could do—wait faithfully and with great expectation.

And then, suddenly, without any warning, the groom would appear in the streets with his groomsmen in tow, all of them calling out in celebration as he marched to claim his betrothed wife. The bridesmaids, hearing the call, would dash to wait with the bride and join her in the bridal party's return procession through the streets toward the wedding ceremony. Afterward, the bride and groom, as well as family and friends, celebrated with a wedding banquet extending for days.

There's that word again—*afterward*.

This image of the ancient Jewish betrothal period is the very one Jesus uses in answer to Peter's pleading, panicked question, "Lord, where are you going?"

Jesus said to Peter, and he says to us: "Let not your hearts be troubled. Believe in God; believe also in me. In my Father's house are many rooms. If it were not so, would I have told you that I go to prepare a place for you? And if I go and prepare a place for you, I will come again and will take you to myself, that where I am you may be also" (John 14:1–3).

Jesus, drawing upon the image of the betrothal period, said we are to wait in faith as a bride waits for her groom, and we are to wait without troubled or anxious hearts. He likens himself to our groom, who has gone away to prepare a dwelling place for us in his Father's house. He's gone away to secure our future, because we are under a binding contract that he himself has guaranteed in blood. In fact, the remaining indwelling Spirit is his etched signature on our hearts, guaranteeing us as Jesus's bride before God.

And so we are the waiting bride. Faith, it seems, is our primary work in the present. We have no idea when our groom will return or when the waiting will come to an end. There is no clear answer to "How long, O Lord?" There is only a promise that "afterward" will eventually come. Jesus is away—we can no longer see his face nor hold his hands nor hear the inflections in his voice—but we have his words, written in contract as if in stone, words that say he's away gathering and cementing the home of our happily ever after—our All Things Beautiful.

The question remains, then: We wait, but do we do so with eager expectation or with troubled and anxious hearts?

Waiting Is Wrestling

I sit at my writing desk and stare out the window. It's late October but most of the leaves still hang on the trees, unchanged from summer. I'm ready for them to fall already, because I've positioned my desk so that when they do, I will be able to see the Blue Ridge Mountains in the distance. I am supposed to be writing, but staring out the window with longing is much easier than doing the difficult work of the present moment—putting fingers to keys. I go to reheat my coffee and check my email before sitting down to stare at my computer and then, having typed nothing, out the window once again. I busy myself with anything and everything but actual writing.

I am, in fact, wrestling, because, if you ask me, writing is a form of wrestling. Wrestling with images and truth and insecurities; trying, in the midst of all those things, to get words on a page that may or may not mean something to someone beyond myself. I try not to panic or think too much about the process but rather simply get words out and evaluate or edit later. Otherwise I'd spend all my writing hours in a fetal position on the carpet, crying hot tears, searching the classifieds for mindless work and trying every which way to slip from under the weight of my deadline.

But I love writing, I really do.

I've embraced how much of writing involves waiting. Waiting for the precise word to pop in my head. Waiting for the story I must tell. Waiting for the puzzle pieces to fall together in a clear picture. Waiting for the message or the imagery that makes my heart pump hard, affirming I'm on the right track. Waiting on God when I much prefer plowing ahead with my own rants and careless words. It's certainly not passive waiting; I'm thinking constantly, attempting to hold thoughts in my head until I can stop the car at a red light and spill them into my Notes app, catching stray thoughts in the margin of my prayer journal, and, yes, sitting down to stare at the computer when I'm not sure where I plan to go with my words. Waiting is active business. Like wrestling, it will make you sweat.

However, the more I've embraced the waiting and the wrestling part of writing, the less I panic and the more I've taken joy in the process. I've learned not to be a taskmaster over myself, pushing and forcing myself harder and harder, because words and ideas can't be forced. The true work of art actually happens in me *in the process* as I wait. The trouble is that I want the joy of having already written, not the unique sort of joy that comes in the middle of the writing process.

Writing is wrestling, but it's mostly waiting and, in the waiting, believing that it's all going to come together somehow in the end to form something beautiful.

I've found that my greatest motivator in wrestle-writing is to envision being done. I imagine holding a completed book in my hands and knowing I gave it everything I could've given in the process. I let it all settle, I considered every word, I worked to connect the disconnected puzzle pieces, I muted my inner negative voice, I wrote as unto God and trusted him to use my meager efforts in some meaningful way. I waited forward, and the waiting was worth it because it moved me along to the most beautiful thing—the completed work. A work of art, however imperfect.

Art, as they say, imitates life. In the Christian life, we're always "in process." As we all do in our own ways, we can try to push ourselves forward, control the process like little mini gods, or worry away all our hours we could instead give toward active faith. We want the joy and the "afterward" without having to wait or wrestle, when in fact the true work of art is being made in us through the very waiting and wrestling we abhor: God is refining and growing our faith.

I was both an impatient girlfriend and an impatient bride-to-be. My husband, Kyle, and I were engaged for seven months prior to our wedding and dated for three years before that, so I was beyond ready to get married. Most of our friends dated, got engaged, and got married during those years of our waiting, and, by the end of our dating period, attending weddings was simply excruciating for me. I wanted it to be my turn. I wanted to wear the white dress and register for gifts and send out invitations. I wanted to plan a wedding and pick out bridesmaid dresses.

And then we got engaged and, somewhat surprisingly, my impatience stayed with me. I had new things to be impatient about: I didn't want to say goodbye to Kyle at night, I wanted to introduce him as my husband rather than my fiancé, and I wanted to go on a honeymoon.

Our wedding day came, we exchanged vows, we went on a honeymoon, we returned to all our new wedding gifts in our little seminary rental house, and, quite suddenly it seemed, I was married. I hadn't prepared for being married as much as I'd planned for the wedding. Of course, one cannot fully prepare for marriage, but in my impatience I'd resisted any process or preparation. I'd waited passively, hoping for the best, when in fact I should've waited actively, learning to embrace the joy in the present moments, a skill which would've served me well in the daily realities of marriage.

Faith is much the same: it is a necessary work for the Christian, because producing saving, enduring faith is God's primary goal for us in the present.

Waiting is not passive; waiting well is extremely hard work, and most of the work is at the heart level. Waiting well means not growing weary and giving up, it means not getting distracted, it means knowing that waiting *is* the work and embracing the wrestling part of it. What enables us to wait and wrestle well is to look forward as a bride does to her wedding day or a writer does to a completed book: look forward to the end and then live in the present in light of that future. We wait forward.

But what exactly are we waiting forward *for*? We are a bride dreaming of her wedding day, which has already been planned for us:

Then I heard what seemed to be the voice of a great multitude, like the roar of many waters and like the sound of mighty peals of thunder, crying out,

"Hallelujah!
For the Lord our God
    the Almighty reigns.
Let us rejoice and exult
    and give him the glory,
for the marriage of the Lamb has come,
    and his Bride has made herself ready;
it was granted her to clothe herself
    with fine linen, bright and pure"—

for the fine linen is the righteous deeds of the saints.
And the angel said to me, "Write this: Blessed are those who are invited to the marriage supper of the Lamb." And he said to me, "These are the true words of God." (Rev. 19:6–9)

And so, the ultimate end we must be confident of is the reward of being with God and enjoying him forever. We will begin our eternal marriage to him with a great big party: the finest food, laughing, dancing, and celebrating. We won't remember tears of sorrow, nor will we remember sin. We won't remember waiting; there will be no need for faith, for faith will be made sight. What had been abstract will take form and substance. Invisible realities will become visible and tangible.

In the present, we are called as Christians to live with hope and joy despite enduring suffering and unjust authorities and standing by as the proud succeed. As John Piper has said, the only way we can do this, the only way hope can be explained, is the sure belief that there is a marriage supper and a reward to come.[3] Waiting forward means living according to paradox kingdom values in preparation and in light of a reality we believe will eventually be. This hope fuels us, enables us, settles us, and also produces a beautiful faith in us in the process of waiting. Hope is the bride making herself ready, with the groom perpetually in her mind.

The groom has gone to make all the preparations, so our work is to wait on him expectantly, as if we're waiting for a work of art to be finished, waiting for that moment when we can stand back and see how the workman has thoughtfully completed his construction. Although we can't see all that he's doing now—how he's putting stone upon stone, building our beautiful end—he is doing invisible work that one day will be made visible.

Do we have an ear cocked, listening for the Groom's returning voice? Do we believe he is coming? Do we anticipate the joy of that moment? Waiting expectantly is the only way we can wrestle our way through the difficulties of life, because our hope is that moment when all our tears and longings will vanish forever.

Stones of Promise

From the moment I got engaged to Kyle, all I could do was stare at the brilliant diamond on my ring finger. Anytime I got in the car to go anywhere, I'd drive with my hands on the top of the steering wheel just so I could gaze at the diamond at every stoplight. Sitting in church, I'd listen to the sermon while simultaneously moving my hand so the bright lights glaring down from the ceiling could catch the diamond and make it sparkle.

I looked at the rock on my finger every chance I could get, partly because I'd never had anything like it in my life but mostly because it represented the promise of what was to come: a wedding day and a marriage.

My engagement ring was and still is a stone of promise.

As we wait for our Groom, God has given us stones to look at: promises of what is to come and what he's doing in the meantime while we wait. Most importantly, perhaps, are the promises made and kept, stones of surety that have been made into altars. They've been erected and scattered throughout time, precisely so we'd see and remember and wait forward with faith.

The flood turned to a rainbow of promise. And then Noah built a stone altar to the Lord, because the Lord had done it.

Hatred and war turned to victory. And then Moses built a stone altar to the Lord, because the Lord had done it.

Sin was atoned for through blood. And then Aaron made sacrifices on the stone altar of the Lord, because the Lord had done it.

A plague birthed from pride was averted. And then David built a stone altar to the Lord, because the Lord had done it.

Jerusalem, the beauty of God, and her exiles were restored from complete rubble and ruin. And then Jeshua and Zerubbabel built an altar to the Lord, because the Lord had done it.[4]

Stones of hope rise up to meet us as we consider who, in the story of time, has been capable of such things. Who has kept promises completely? Who's given victory in war? Who has held the ability to forgive sins? Who's restored what seemed forever in disrepair? Who's turned death to life?

Whose work brought repentant prostitutes and idol-worshipers into the family tree of Jesus? Whose work made the barren full with child? Who ordered nations and people and rulers to certain places at certain times for specific purposes? Who caused a Persian king to lose sleep, setting in motion the salvation of an entire people group?[5]

This Builder is the same one you know. Stone upon stone—and he is still building a work of art with us. We see the incomplete construction, but we can look at what's already complete so we might wait well.

What is undone is wrenching. There are altars yet to be built and some that hold our greatest pain, and we are surrendered and yet squirming in unrest and uncertainty.

Even those who see Jesus face-to-face are waiting while holding their longings: "When he opened the fifth seal, I saw under the altar the souls of those who had been slain for the word of God and for the witness they had borne. They cried out with a loud voice, 'O Sovereign Lord, holy and true, how long?'" (Rev. 6:9–10).

Peter said, "How long?"

The martyrs say, "How long?"

And we, waiting, cry, "How long?"

He is not done yet. We all cry out for justice, for all things to be made right and beautiful. This is, in fact, the very story he's writing. He is not ordering time and moving nations like chess pieces just for order's sake or for fun; he's building toward our All Things Beautiful. Stone by stone, he's gathering beauty together.

So we must take up our post as the bride waiting for her groom with unwavering faith, straining to hear his voice, and knowing we wait because there are more he wants to invite to the marriage supper.

Present Promises

I paint my toenails in bright swaths of pink and instruct myself as a mother might her child: sit still and let the polish dry. I slouch on the side of the tub, look at my toes, and wait for a full ten or fifteen seconds before hurrying off to blow dry my hair and put the laundry away, convincing myself that I will remember not to let my toes touch anything. I step carefully as I go, but within seconds I've forgotten. And then, of course, the polish gets smudged or I put on shoes too early and feel the stickiness of the polish, and only then do I remember.

I have little patience and am far too easily distracted; I'm not sure I know how to actively wait for the polish to dry.

Oh, but this very skill is needed in the Christian life, because the Christian life is all about waiting. Waiting on God for direction. Waiting on God to answer a prayer we've prayed for decades. Waiting on the Groom to return. The New Testament writers run out of ways to exhort us: endure, persevere, be patient, don't give up, don't fall away.

Wait, they seem to say, for the work of art that is the redemption story to be complete. The paint is not yet dry. Don't judge the Artist's work prematurely.

As Matthew Henry says,

We must wait with patience for the full discovery of that which to us seems intricate and perplexed, acknowledging that we cannot find out the work that God makes from the beginning to the end, and therefore must judge nothing before the time. We are to believe that God has made all beautiful. Every thing is done well, as in creation, so in providence, and we shall see it when the end comes, but till then we are incompetent judges of it.[6]

In other words, don't get up from the side of the bathtub, because beauty is building.

Others, frustrated with waiting, have found ways to cast stones at a God they say is not there. They, in the midst of pain, are in a fetal position on the floor, looking for any other way. Instead of building altars of remembrance, they use their stones to cast lots, trying to find out the plan from beginning to end. They cast stones of premature judgment: *certainly this cannot ever be beautiful; look at what it is right now!*

That's what the rejecters did: they spurned the Cornerstone. They wanted another way—the world to be made right in front of their eyes, for them, for their children, in their time. They didn't want slow, meticulous building upon this Stone.

Our world rejects him too, for these very reasons.

Do we?

There is no other way. Beauty is building and will only come through waiting. Let us not judge prematurely with blinded eyes, as the world does, for "the world has not only gained possession of the heart, but has formed prejudices there against the beauty of God's works."[7]

Why not look at what we can see and know? We've got stones of promise we can look at every day.

And he says he is preparing a place for us in heaven and will come back for us. He says there is a wedding celebration coming.

The promises we make are imperfect, but his promises are sure and steadfast. Our faith in him is never misplaced, for he keeps his word perfectly. Has he redeemed you from your enslavement to sin? Has he healed your broken heart? Has he placed you in a family when you were a spiritual or biological orphan? Has he brought your prodigal home? Has he enabled you to forgive the unforgivable? Has he helped you endure an unwanted circumstance and even given you joy in it? Has he used a trial to give you deeper faith? Write down his faithfulness, so you may recall it often and share it with those in earshot.

God has not fixed all of our inconsolable things. Even when we've experienced redemption, we find difficulty. When an affair is forgiven, there is still much to work through. When an unbelieving spouse bows to Christ, the marriage must shift and evolve. When unwanted singleness continues on without end and it's embraced as a sacrificial joy, one must continue to fight for contentment. When a prodigal child returns, the consequences of sin still follow.

However, these altars tell us all we need to know: God exists, he is working just out of sight, and he has not forgotten the promises he's made to his bride. Our stories are brush-strokes on the canvas displaying the redemption story—his story. We must wait for the paint to dry.

The Completed Work

From my writing desk, I see the FedEx truck careen onto my street and stop at the base of my driveway. I've been told the page proofs of my book are coming today, and I know instinctively this person in the big white truck is bringing me what's been promised. I jump out of my chair and do a little happy dance, expectantly awaiting the moment when I tear open the envelope and hold the pages in my hand. I will finally see the final work—the actual book. I'll see the font the graphic designer has chosen, the way the chapter titles are placed on the page, and the exact number of pages all my work ended up becoming.

I'll finally hold it in my hands.

All that work. I put my heart, mental energy, my everything into those words.

And in that moment of doing a happy dance next to my writing desk, I've forgotten all the times I lay awake at night, worried, or the times I believed I couldn't actually complete it. I've forgotten the sheer panic and the profound insecurities. I've forgotten the burden of the deadlines and the times I searched the classifieds for a mindless job.

I've forgotten it all, because the work is complete.

Or maybe it's that I'm thankful because there was beauty even in the process, beauty that came *from* the process. The most beautiful things come only through perseverance and waiting: hope and character and, above all, a beautiful unwavering faith. The most beautiful saints are those who have lived through the gore of life with an eye on the beauty to come. What crowns they will wear.

All the work of waiting will be worth it when we hear the voice of the Groom calling to us from the streets.

I run to the door to meet the FedEx guy, just as one day we, the Bride, will run to Jesus.

I can't wait to see.

God Is Our Color

He Paints Beauty When We Pursue Holiness

> For everything there is a season, and a time for
> every matter under heaven: *a time to embrace,
> and a time to refrain from embracing.*

I LACE UP MY WALKING SHOES and head out into the unseasonably warm November morning without a jacket. I've waited and waited for the autumn leaves to turn their brilliant shades but the fall has been hotter and drier than usual, so the trees are clinging greedily to their leaves, and the leaves themselves are stubbornly refusing to turn. I take the pine-needled path from our neighborhood to the next one, a familiar walk that gives my mind freedom to churn and daydream. Coming out of the path, I'm suddenly jolted out of my reverie by a straight-backed maple tree reaching for the sky with armfuls of blazing red leaves, a show-off tree that stops me in my tracks. From trunk to tip, the tree appears on fire, its beauty accentuated by a backdrop of crisp blue sky and happy green leaves from neighboring trees on both sides. I try to drink it in, imprinting it on my memory, searching for the exact color of red I'd label these leaves.

Crimson.

No, the leaves are brighter than that. Cherry red, maybe. But there is a hint of orange, almost neon in shade.

The wind suddenly blows through, shaking the branches until leaves release and float down, and I want to stand beneath it and hold the leaves on, to somehow straightjacket the branches, prevent the inevitable, and still the wind. The leaves will be gone altogether soon enough. After they pile on the ground beneath the tree, exchanging their red for a dull tint of faded brown, someone will come and rake them up or blow them away entirely.

I realize then what I'd name the shade of the leaves I'm staring at: Pure Red. It's as if they've each been dipped all the way to their stems in the starkest red dye I can imagine.

After a few minutes of standing in a stranger's yard with my face toward the sky, I turn toward home. Retracing my steps down the pine-needled path, I look back one last time at my Pure Red maple tree so that I might hold its exact color in my mind. At a distance, it stands surrounded by dozens of other trees, few of which bear standout leaves like my maple. Some display the occasional yellow leaf or patch of deep red or pastel orange mixed in among the basic green, but my eye is drawn solely to the maple. She is fully and completely dressed for glory.

In the fall, it's the pure ones that are the prettiest.

Dipped in Christ

We too are dipped in color—those of us who have followed Jesus by faith. We are dipped in Jesus himself: "For as many of you as were baptized into Christ have put on Christ" (Gal. 3:27).

What color are we, then? If we are draped in him, covered by him, dyed by him, what invisible hues do we unknowingly live and move and have our being in every day? If we were to stand before him as I did my maple, dazzled by his colors, what might our eyes take in?

The disciple John, in the revelation given to him by God, described whom he saw seated on the throne of heaven—Jesus—like this: "And he who sat there had the appearance of jasper and carnelian, and around the throne was a rainbow that had the appearance of an emerald" (Rev. 4:3). Jasper and carnelian are types of quartz, typically shaded red, while emerald is, of course, a green gem. Note, however, that John said Jesus had the *appearance* of these things. It's as if he can't quite find words precise enough to describe him; John has nothing he can truly compare with what he saw. He can only say Jesus had the appearance of bright colors, helping us understand that, although indescribable, he is beautiful, dazzling, and surrounded by a relative to our rainbow.

What John is absolutely certain about the Godhead is his holiness. He overhears the elders and creatures surrounding the throne chanting, "Holy, holy, holy, is the Lord God Almighty, who was and is and is to come!"

We don't know the precise colors he wears; we only know they are pure, because he himself is pure and holy.

In regard to art and colors, *purity* is defined as the chroma, saturation, and degree from white of any given color.[1] A pure color means it's all of one with no others mixed in, free from anything that debases or contaminates. There is no modifying addition. As soon as a pure color is mixed with another, it becomes something entirely different, something polluted from its original, something of lesser beauty.

The Godhead is holy. Nothing in him has been debased or contaminated: no sin, no wrong motive or evil intent. He is all good, always. God's color, then, is Pure.

Ours certainly isn't. We all have contaminated, impure hearts gifted to us by Adam and Eve. Our hearts deceive us, condemn us, and fixate us on self-interest at all costs. And the cost of this pollution is death.

The cross of Christ beckons with life and breath, a strong and safe refuge for those who know their need. Through faith in Jesus we've been dipped into him and come out covered in his color—Pure—all the way down to the heart. This is, in essence, what 2 Corinthians 5:21 proclaims: "For our sake he made him to be sin who knew no sin, so that in him we might become the righteousness of God."

When we embrace Christ, he covers us like clothing. Because of this—because God looks at us dipped and robed in Christ—we're blazingly beautiful in God's sight. We're considered pure as Christ is pure; we're free from the curse of sin because Christ won freedom for us by taking the curse himself. All is settled, for always.

And so we have been given this gift that can't be taken away—no longer are we regarded and identified by our skin color or our hair color but are defined and identified by his unseen colors of jasper and carnelian and emerald. It's no longer we who live but Christ who lives in us, bursting forth from our hearts with indescribable color and compelling us to honor the one who's given such a gift.[2]

The truth of this gift can be difficult to see and challenging to fully comprehend. Sometimes the words we use to describe our faith blur our comprehension further. We often speak of a belief in Christ, as if it's merely a cerebral assent to the truths and ideas of who Christ is and what he did for us. However, as Sinclair Ferguson says,

> The benefits of the gospel are *in Christ. They do not exist apart from him.* They are *ours* only *in him.* They cannot be abstracted from him as if we ourselves could possess them independently of him. New Testament Christians did not think of themselves as "Christians"! But if not, how did they think of themselves? Contrast these descriptors with the overwhelmingly dominant way the New Testament describes believers. It is that we are "in Christ." The expression, in one form or another, occurs well over one hundred times in Paul's thirteen letters. Then draw the obvious conclusion: If this is not the overwhelmingly dominant way in which we think about ourselves, we are not thinking with the renewed mind of the gospel.[3]

We must consider ourselves "in Christ," which gives us a picture of our lives being a drop of water inside a vast ocean. We are swallowed up by Christ's grace, love, and purity; his grace far exceeds our sin, and we cannot think of ourselves as somehow apart from him.

In this in-between, we wait to see this freedom by sight, and as we wait, our old lives call out to us quite often and quite loudly with one mantra: *If we are dipped in purity that cannot be removed, why does it matter how we live in this in-between?* The end of the story seems assured, and we know we're forgiven, so why does obedience even matter? This is what our human wisdom and fleshly desires want us to question, and, in fact, our old way of life tempts us by holding up pollution and calling it beautiful freedom, coaxing us back.

Why *does* it matter how we live?

First and foremost, a pure life points to a coming kingdom and its coming King. Following the cry of, "Holy, holy, holy," the elders and living creatures exemplify the only right response in light of God's purity: "Worthy are you, our Lord and God, to receive glory and honor and power, for you created all things, and by your will they existed and were created" (Rev. 4:11).

The Bible says that, as Christians, we are to live lives of holiness and godliness in honor of this King.[4] "For God did not call us to be impure, but to live a holy life" (1 Thess. 4:7 NIV). This doesn't mean we're to pursue being right with God; if we've embraced Jesus by faith we've already been dipped in Christ and are seen as perfectly right in the sight of God. What it does mean is that we're to actively refrain from embracing pollutants that mar our gifted purity and, in doing so, mar our own freedom. Embracing purity as a way of life is for our own beauty and our own good, and it reflects the unseen reality that we're dipped in Christ. The cross of Christ not only beckons and dips but also by nature seeps and soaks into every piece of us. Purity is who we are, so why would we act in accordance to what we are no longer?

Take, for example, the apostle Paul's illustration of polluting ourselves with sexual sin in 1 Corinthians 6:15–18:

Do you not know that your bodies are members of Christ? Shall I then take the members of Christ and make them members of a prostitute? Never! Or do you not know that he who is joined to a prostitute becomes one body with her? For as it is written, "The two will become one flesh." But he who is joined to the Lord becomes one spirit with him. Flee from sexual immorality.

Paul warns us, not because God is a cosmic Goody-Two-Shoes or because he wants to withhold a beautiful gift from us but because by embracing sin, we in effect lead Christ into situations where pollutants blur his glory.

When we lead Christ into these situations—into sexual immorality, human degradation, hatred, or greed—we not only dishonor the gift he's given us but we take away our own joy. We choose in those moments to embrace the old ways, which effectually make us blind and lost again, unable to see good and beauty for what they are. We lose the clarity to determine what is true beauty and what is fleeting, harmful beauty. We also can't taste true freedom when we're engaging impurities that reintroduce the consequences of our old ways—guilt, condemnation, awakened evil desires. All of this takes us away from the knowledge and understanding of the love of the Father, so we run and hide from him rather than running *to* him. Embracing impurity is a primary means of running from beauty.

Paintbrushes

The leaves are now falling far too quickly for my liking, so I lace up my walking shoes and go again to gaze at my Pure

Red maple tree before she's lost her leaves entirely. Once again I drink in the color, memorizing every contour, that I may recall it in the dreary, colorless days of winter and enliven my own heart.

I take notice of the trees around the maple. Finally, they also are turning, in imitation of their neighbor. Their leaves remain green except at the tips, where their transformation has begun; there, closest to the sun, they are various shades of yellow and orange and maroon.

For the first time, I see that the trees resemble brushes dipped in paint: brown trunks as handles, branches formed as bristles, and the uppermost leaves as the artist's chosen color. Each tree a paintbrush dipped in a color of fall.

And suddenly I think of God wielding his power in this world not as a forceful hammer or a demanding thunderbolt but as an artist's paintbrush dipped in the purity of his people.

I see then that God paints beauty with purity. We are paintbrushes being transformed as we present ourselves, branches wide, to the Son. God then paints with our lives, dipping into our vivid purity and sweeping broad strokes across the canvas of this world. I speak of the Artist with my life when I'm submitted into his hands, embracing obedience as the beautiful way.

This is, in fact, the way we embrace him and unwrap the purity he's given us—we obey him. We refrain from embracing what defames him. Purity is not simply something we're dipped in; it is also what we're purified to do. We live according to who we are because the great gift compels us but also so that we may remain transparent and let his jasper and carnelian and emerald shine through.

We were made pure to live pure. This is how the Holy One can receive glory and honor from our lives, and how others see his beauty.

Learning obedience is one purpose for this in-between waiting period. It's why God asks us to wait for the resolution of a difficult circumstance. It's one reason why God allows suffering in our lives and why there are inconsolable things among us. Jesus himself learned obedience through suffering.[5] He was perfectly obedient before his Father, but as a human being, his time and work on earth were completed through his submission to suffering.

If Jesus, though perfect, endured purposeful suffering as a form of obedience, how much more must we commit ourselves to learning and pursuing obedience? This is costly obedience, because it means refusing to embrace our old ways and what our very desires may tell us to do. But in the end embracing purity is choosing the vivid, colorful way of life. Only in refraining from embracing mixtures that don't belong do we keep the purity of our color intact.

Obedience shines back on him, but it is also for our joy. This, too, is a gift of God, that he would give purpose to our obedience but also birth fruit from it for our benefit.

As I stand under my Pure Red maple, the sun spreads out in a crisp blue sky, the breeze tickles the leaves, and I smile and close my eyes. Really, I want to raise my hands and lift my face toward the sun and sing at the top of my lungs. That's what a little beauty will do. But I'm in a stranger's yard in the middle of the day, so I instead take a deep breath and ingest the warmth and the color like air. All of it together makes me incredibly happy.

This is what obedience feels like.

Purity Looks Forward

It also feels like dying.

As I stand beneath my maple, it's a glorious day, but the leaves, I must not forget, are a portrait of death. As if to underscore this truth, a single crimson leaf draws my attention as it releases from a high branch and floats through the air like an acrobat. Landing softly on the ground, it will soon grow brittle and decay and be swept away.

However, in its short life, it has served its purpose well. This little leaf turned red in order to help the tree prepare for winter. As chlorophyll exits maples, the red color, called anthocyanin, appears as a sort of sunscreen, buying time so that the leaf can transfer nutrients to the tree's roots it will need during dormant months. The leaf gives its life—every last nutrient—for the furtherance of the tree. Without this quick outfit change from green to red, the leaf would be susceptible to light damage as it literally takes itself apart to give life to the tree.[6]

This is both a portrait of death and a portrait of incredible beauty.

Obedience works much the same way. Embracing God and pursuing his ways means a refraining from self—his honor and fame are furthered when we die to ourselves and live to him. Because obedience is a type of death, it can be excruciating, uncomfortable, and raw. It can leave us feeling exposed, fragile, and shaky, like the last leaf swinging on the tree branch. Often, we must fight terribly hard to resist temptation, sit in the discomfort of the crucified flesh's last gasps, and do all of it without promise of immediate benefit.

Unlike the little red leaf, however, our sacrifice is not swept away or forgotten. Rather, it is greatly rewarded by God himself, who sees all. He honors those who give away their lives in order to honor him.

How does he do this?

As the anthocyanin protects the leaf, God has designed obedience as a protection against some forms of suffering, specifically self-inflicted suffering that results from sin. Our disobedience breeds preventable guilt, preventable consequences or circumstances, and preventable discipline. Disobedience puts us in situations that swing wide the door for addiction, harm, or bondage. As walking on the sidewalk instead of the street protects us from some dangers, our obedience lessens opportunities for suffering. Of course, not all suffering is a direct result of disobedience, but some certainly is. Suffering in this life is guaranteed, so why compound it through disobedience?

The apostle Peter draws on Psalm 34 when he says,

Whoever desires to love life and see good days, let him keep his tongue from evil and his lips from speaking deceit; let him turn away from evil and do good; let him seek peace and pursue it. For the eyes of the Lord are on the righteous, and his ears are open to their prayer. But the face of the Lord is against those who do evil. (1 Pet. 3:10–12)

God, it seems, rewards obedience with peace, but there is a lesson we must learn from the little red leaf: the obedience of self-death is primarily rewarded later. The tree doesn't bear witness to what nutrients the leaf has passed on until spring. In the winter, nothing worthwhile seems to have happened; all is bare and seemingly barren.

I know a woman who has considered leaving her marriage. She is not unsafe in it, but she has not always been happy. She stays, believing that honoring God through her obedience is better in the long run for her and for her family.

And it is.

I imagine that her choice to forgive, to work, to cultivate, to choose truth over emotion is growing up a sturdy tree in her home. Her children sit under a red maple in summer, safe and happy, although they don't know what it's taken to grow that tree. They are rewarded with beauty and protective shade through her obedience, she is rewarded with God's peace, and future generations will be rewarded in ways they won't even know.

It doesn't feel like a blue-sky, red-leaf day when we're faced with the choice of which we will embrace, self or God. Nor when we go against our own flesh to choose God. But after we have chosen to obey, God, with his paintbrush, swirls up an inexplicable joy in our hearts. Not because the circumstances change or the strain of temptation eases. Not because our flesh has finally been vanquished. Only because we've lived according to who we are, and God, a proud Father, has drawn near. There is a singularly beautiful color reserved for obedience that colors our hearts with peace.

God then paints beauty by wielding a paintbrush covered in purity within our homes, our relationships, our workplaces, and all across the canvas of this world.

I want more for this woman in her marriage. I want fulfillment and happiness. I pray her obedience bears greater fruit in this life. I pray God helps her emotions fall in line behind her choice, but I know for certain that her obedience will be rewarded in the further future—in heaven. This is the certain outcome of obedience, and it's a form of saving up for later. It's the athlete forgoing leisure because of practice, the farmer forgoing rest for work, the mother forgoing her child's immediate pleasure in order to discipline, and the leaf forgoing its life for the furtherance of the tree. All of these things are done with the future in mind.

Our obedience must be motivated by God's face in the future. Because we will see him, because he will make all things beautiful, we can believe that joy will come in the spring, that all of our unseen self-deaths were seen all along and will be rewarded by God himself.

This is what motivated Christ's self-death. Christ didn't obey his Father because he felt like it; in fact, his emotions told him to look for a way out. He also didn't obey because it was easy; in fact, it cost him dearly. He obeyed for the "joy that was set before him," namely a seat of honor in the presence of his Father, and so he might bring "many sons to glory."[7]

When we obey, we imitate and honor him. Our obedience, like his, will be pointed in the direction of the Father and will be an invitation for others to know him. And, like him, there is joy set before us: "And after you have suffered a little while, the God of all grace, who has called you to his eternal glory in Christ, will himself restore, confirm, strengthen, and establish you" (1 Pet. 5:10).

When I stand on the heater grate in my kitchen in the dead of winter, my one hope is that spring is coming. I can't see it. I can only look forward, believing the leaf has done its job.

Vivid Living

I wake my boys early on a Saturday morning for our appointment with the photographer. I cajole and coax and finally command them into clothes they would rather not wear for pictures they would rather not take. After dressing, they stand in the kitchen side-by-side, reluctantly allowing my comb through their hair, questioning for the hundredth time why we are up so early.

The morning light is best, I tell them, repeating what the photographer explained to me.

We go to the park, the one with the mountains in the background, and stand as we're told against the rustic fence. We smile dutifully, at least some of us. My words seem set on loop: "Boys, stand up straight. Look at the camera. Smile. Smile *normally*."

We try to appear decent and well-groomed—for one hour, at least.

Although there is much complaining and gnashing of teeth, they do it all for me. My husband, too, who cares little about beautiful family photos, does it for me. He knows I want the pictures for the entry in our home and for Christmas cards and gifts for grandparents. He will want them, too, no matter how reluctant he is, because they will stay with us long after this torturous morning, and we will study them together year after year, searching out details of how the boys have grown.

That's why I want family pictures. I want to remember my boys at these ages, when they stood stair-step next to one another, when my oldest had braces, when my middle son was on the verge of turning eleven, when my youngest still had a sort of "little boy" to him. That's why we are at the park early on a Saturday—because I want a sunlight strong enough to point out every detail so I may keep those details forever. I want to capture the beauty of this moment in time.

I want vivid color, and the morning sunlight will well reproduce bright reds and blues and greens in the photographs.

The photographer, in order to capture the colors and details I want, must consider the light because of saturation. Harsh, bright light will overexpose the photograph, while too little light will underexpose. Pure, vivid colors come with a perfectly light-saturated exposure. And pure, vivid colors are dazzling.

This is grace that leads to holy living: knowing the light of the Father's love. His is a love that never shames nor guilts us into obedience. It's the grace that came for us, that went first in sacrifice, that opened a relationship to us. And it's the grace that teaches and instructs and loves enough to discipline.

Living obedient to God, motivated by his love, is vivid living—the most colorful way to live.

We too often think of obedience to God and our pursuit of holiness as *keeping* us from color and life and beauty. The words we use to describe right and wrong are black and white, and if we're generous with our boundaries, gray. Instead, obedience is bright orange and joyful yellow and warm turquoise—really any pure color—because obedience is more worshipful, joyful gratitude than anything else. Obedience is the reflexive song of the free; it actually helps us fully receive and embrace the freedom we've been given in Christ.

At the moment our faith was placed in Christ, we were dipped in him and the truest of true realities became true for us: we are now seen as perfect in God's eyes because we're covered all over in Christ. God knows this reality, but it often takes time for us to come to an understanding of it. Our minds need transforming, our hearts need disciplining, our lives need to be split open by the Holy Spirit. God is patient to take one step at a time, knowing to do otherwise would crush us. Only in presenting ourselves to God can the truth of who we've become in Christ become move vivid and real to us. As we do so, the Holy Spirit gives us the mind of Christ, the perspective of God, and the ability to continue pursuing purity. We begin to recognize the beauty in patient endurance and costly obedience, and not only do we recognize it but we begin to *crave* God's incisive work on us.

As we wait for God's answers in God's timing, let us live as dipped in Christ. Let us sit as a wick in the wisdom of Scripture each day, letting who we already are seep in more and more, letting ourselves be trained under the authority of God's Word.

This way of wisdom grows us up, not as a pure red maple but as a strong oak, ablaze with the beauty grown from letting our roots sink deeper and deeper in the understanding of what it means to be dipped in Pure Christ.[8]

This is transforming beauty while waiting for ultimate beauty, and it's the most vivid life there is.

If you want beauty, then what you really want is purity.

Dear heart, it's only when you embrace God and refrain from embracing self that you'll discover this to be true. The scales will fall from your eyes and the world will come alive, beauty all around. Purity gives you eyes to see it and to appreciate it. Instead of fear, you'll find the beauty in winter. Instead of lack, you'll find fullness and provision. Instead of barrenness, you'll know life. Instead of little deaths, you'll see future resurrection. Instead of sacrifice, you'll see reward. Although you'll see winter with your eyes, you'll experience spring in your heart.

But in the fall?

In the fall you must remember: it's the pure ones that are the prettiest.

God Is an Author

He Writes Beautiful Stories with Our Weaknesses

> For everything there is a season, and a time for
> every matter under heaven: *a time to seek, and
> a time to lose; a time to keep, and a time to cast
> away; a time to tear, and a time to sew.*

IN OUR FAMILY, we have a recurring conversation about which superhero is best. My oldest says Spider-Man because he has the ability to produce spiderwebs from his wrists and swing from buildings, and that's pretty cool.

My husband prefers Superman, because he can fly and lift buildings and has eyes that can laser things. (But why, he wonders aloud, does Clark Kent feel the need to hold down a stressful day job? He's Superman, for crying out loud.)

I place my vote for Batman, mainly because I know it will send my boys into a tizzy, ranting about how Batman really has no superhero powers at all, only a gadget-filled car and an impressive outfit. I have no real interest in this conversation (see also: *Star Wars*), but I do actually prefer Batman, because the introvert in me wishes I could be like him: dark and brooding and hidden away in a cave where no one bothers me except when I'm needed for a few moments of heroic brilliance. And I also wouldn't mind the twenty-four-hour butler service.

After many discussions, we've realized how much our choice for best superhero comes down to their weaknesses. Spiderman's weakness, as my husband has astutely pointed out, is that he requires tall buildings in order to do his best work, which limits his heroism to urban areas. I also think about how he's a slight, nerdy high school student with anger issues, but I don't say this out loud. My boys don't like Batman because, despite wearing a flowing cape, he can't fly. Ironman's power depends solely on that blinking light thingy in his chest cavity, and Superman loses all his strength at the slightest whiff of kryptonite.

I suppose even superheroes must have their weaknesses, because their stories wouldn't be interesting without them. A compelling story usually involves a character who wants something and overcomes conflict to get it, so weaknesses are unfortunate and sometimes tragic but they're also an essential element to the conflict of any story.[1] Without their flaws or weaknesses, superheroes would have no obstacles to overcome, and, as the audience, we wouldn't enjoy any climactic or suspenseful moments. We'd feel no sense of satisfaction and finality when our favorite superheroes win in the end.

And they always do win in the end. This is why I can close my eyes for a catnap or daydream during an action movie, which I do quite often during the endless car/motorcycle/helicopter chase scenes. I already know what's going to happen—there seems to be a sort of template for these movies—so I have no need to worry about the protagonist's well-being while my eyes are closed. When I open my eyes, he or she will still be standing, still be fighting, and, yes, still be living with their identity-defining weakness, because a sequel is coming soon.

Although a superhero's weakness makes for a good story, we don't like how much weakness defines who we are in real life.

On a recent Monday I stayed in my pajamas until 4:00 p.m. Although I woke up early and drank two back-to-back cups of coffee, the fuzz of sleep didn't burn away until late morning. By that point, showering and changing into clothes felt a bit too strenuous, so I didn't force the issue with myself. Instead of choosing hygiene, I chose to do a lot of staring off into space, giving my brain a chance to think again after a whirlwind of activity the previous week.

Why is it that when my body is exhausted, my mind goes into overdrive? As I lay in bed, staring, taking a moment in my room to get my act together, my thoughts began berating me. For being tired. For feeling the need to rest. For not having the mental or physical capacity to immediately move on to the "next thing" on my agenda.

I immediately did what I always attempt to do—I tried forcing myself through the tiredness. This never works, although I still try it every time. However, instead of helping, trying to force myself only makes me more tired and much grumpier. It's almost as if I get mad at myself for being weak.

We don't like reminders that we're limited. We wrestle with our weaknesses, trying to eradicate them completely. We hide them from others and even have trouble admitting them to ourselves. We're driven to prove ourselves sufficient. Case in point: I feel the need to tell you that said Monday was a national holiday. I feel the need to tell you that staying in my pajamas until 4:00 p.m. is a rare occurrence, a very rare occurrence. I feel the need to prove my life is in constant motion, because I'm capable! I'm self-sufficient! I'm dependable! (*Said proudly as she changes into her superhero cape.*)

And then I get a glimpse of myself in the mirror. I see the wrinkles, the gray hairs, the flab where there used to be muscle. My body is aging; death is somewhere out there, coming for me. In the mirror is a physical reminder of a spiritual truth: there is no superhero here. I am a dependent being, not a self-sufficient one, and my ever-increasing limits push me down toward the dirt from which I was formed. I will never be able to climb up and escape the dirt, never reach the place of God, never fully overcome my weaknesses or my limits.

I thought I was the superhero, but in fact there must be another.

This is the conclusion the apostle Paul came to when he prayed for release from his unnamed weakness. God said to him that the power of God is fully present in man's weakness, so Paul responded, "I will boast all the more gladly of my weaknesses, so that the power of Christ may rest upon me" (2 Cor. 12:9).

Paul didn't try to overcome his weaknesses, nor did he hide them. He embraced his weaknesses as opportunities for the beauty of God to grow and display itself in his life.

He trusted that God could somehow do something with and through the weaknesses.

In admitting and embracing our weaknesses and limits, we recognize that Jesus is the hero of the story, and he's a hero who overcame the weakness of his human frailty for us so we might overcome sin and death too. He is limitless and he offers to act on our behalf in our limited state. We must seek to exalt him and his abilities and lose whatever hero status we think we can attain. We must live as the dependent beings we are.

It is in allowing our weakness to push us toward the dirt, toward self-death, that we find beauty resides at the bottom. We find, in death, resurrection and life. So we must not be afraid of the little daily deaths when we cannot, in our self-sufficiency, rescue and deliver and throw off this flesh.

This is the redemption story—death and resurrection—and it's the template story God authors over and over.

Paul's cry, then, must be ours: *God, author me. Be the hero in my weakness. Write resurrection with my self-death.*

Little Deaths, Little Resurrections

Perhaps something you've feared has come to fruition or something's been torn apart in your life. Where have your weaknesses and limits been exacerbated? How has your heart been broken? Where do you feel helpless and hopeless?

These are the little deaths where God wants to author resurrection life in the present. Because his story—his template—is restoration. Not all of our trials and difficulties are inconsolable things; some trials will not conclude until all things are made beautiful, but some will see their conclusion before heaven. All are meant to solidify our faith.

God is a sort of screenwriter, and he's been writing the same story over and over and over again since Adam and Eve. The script even seems to have been written as eternity on our hearts: we resonate with the underdog; we want everything that's tilted to be set straight, every jilted lover to find true love, every injustice to be brought before an honorable court, every uncertainty to be made clear, every problem to find its resolution, every person to find their freedom, and every obstacle to fall. We want to see, in the end, that all of the blood, sweat, and tears were worth it. Even our romance and action movies involve a form of redemption, because in movies that follow the typical script, love and good and peace win in the end.

In one of my favorite books, *Peace Child*, author Don Richardson writes about his missionary work among a primitive people untouched by modern civilization. Their tribes were wrecked with betrayal, murder, and cannibalism, all considered the highest of virtues in their cultural code. After years of learning the tribal language, Richardson finally knew enough to share the story of Jesus with the people he'd grown to love. As soon as Judas entered the telling of the story, however, the tribal men erupted in celebration—the best betrayer was always celebrated and emulated. Richardson had to find a new way within the template of the culture to share the gospel, where they could understand Jesus was the hero instead of Judas. He waited, observed, and continued to live among the tribes. One day, after especially harrowing fighting between the people, he watched as two families from rival and warring tribes exchanged their own children in order to pardon murderous acts and make lasting peace. Finally, he saw the redemption story that had been woven among the culture for generations, and he used this Peace Child ceremony to show what Jesus had done for them in a way they understood.

God has and is writing billions of scripts just like this across generations and cultures. In fact, he's writing right now with each of us, and all of them are redemption stories. We're the story within the larger story, and in the larger story, the Hero wins in the end. Therefore we are, by way of the Hero, victors.

But the way of the victor is not what we think of as beautiful. The way of the victor is down on our knees in the dirt, in humility and in complete dependence on Another. The way of the victor is depending on the Strong.

That day, when I stayed in my pajamas until 4:00, instead of berating myself to climb up, I decided to ride my limits down toward dependence. I simply prayed, asking for the Lord to remind me of what's true about him, and therefore how his limitlessness lifts my head.

The first thing he brought to my mind was his faithfulness. I was tired *precisely* because of his faithfulness, which sounds funny to say but it's true. I ticked back through the previous days and thought about what each had entailed: a meal with friends whom God had used us to pursue for years, a women's retreat where dear women shared stories of how God had redeemed and healed them, our Sunday church gathering with so many beloved people built into a healthy community by God, and a wedding of someone I love who had faithfully endured tremendous pain.

And that was only the weekend.

As I ticked back before that in my mind, I found instance upon instance of how I'd encountered and experienced God's faithfulness. I was tired because I had been thrown around in a pinball machine of God's goodness.

The second truth he brought to mind was that I was tired because I am tire-able. I am able to tire. I am limited *by design*. When I get mad at myself because I've run up against the borders of my humanity and try to force myself through those limits by valiantly pushing on toward the "next thing," I hinder God's power showing through my weakness.

I was starting to see what God was trying to say to me:

God = limitless goodness and faithfulness
Me = limited in every way
God-designed limits for me = God's goodness
and faithfulness to me

How was this can't-get-out-of-my-pjs weariness God's goodness to me? He was offering me time and space not only to rest but also to *remember*. Of course limits help us in myriad ways, but the main one is that if we didn't have limits, we would never stop. If we didn't stop, we wouldn't take time to recall what God has done or to reflect on his goodness. Limits are gifts that help us remember that our greatest gift is a God who is limitless.

My mind cleared in those truths, and my heart settled back in peace. I don't have to force myself through limits, nor do I have to listen to the self-condemnation I'm so prone to berate myself with. I can, in fact, let my limits direct me toward dependence. And I can, in fact, receive a pajama day as a gracious gift from God, because as I lose myself in him, he provides for me, he cares for me, he protects me, and he strengthens me.

He writes.

Shared Costs

We face far more difficult things in this life than being tired, things that make us doubt if God is authoring anything at all, much less a beautiful redemption story. We have, after all, an enemy who prowls around like a roaring lion looking for any opening in which to attack and devour us.

Contrary to what we think, a lion doesn't attack the weak and dependent. He attacks those who are staunchly independent, who have wandered from the herd.

Those who know they are limited and dependent beings are not only driven toward their limitless and powerful God but are also driven toward those who tell of him with their lives: the church. The herd.

A herd of animals welcomes the weak into its most secure parts: to protect them, to nurture them, to heal them.

We, too, must cast away our independence and keep company with the redeemed so that we may hear the stories of how resurrection life has come from self-death and we may have hope that our story will be the same.

We must hear that there are the self-deaths before the beauty. In other words, there are costs.

Rosaria Butterfield has said, "The cross is ruthless."[2] There is ruthlessness between the cross and an unconverted person but the cross is equally relentless toward the converted. This latter relentlessness—how the cross requires us daily to come and die to self and live to God—is something I've not always understood. Nonetheless, the cross has been relentless in my life, pursuing and crucifying my claims of self-rule and self-glory. The gospel, because it is by nature sacrificial, requires my self-sacrifice. We don't get the beautiful redemption story without first losing all to gain it.

The gospel lays claim to us all. Christ lays claim to our ambitions, our money, our minds, our work, our children, and our sexual activity. We cannot lay out for the unconverted a Christianity that will "make life better," when in fact faith in Jesus often makes life more difficult because the priceless value of knowing him comes at a cost to self. We become no longer our own; everything we are and do must be submitted to someone else—namely Christ.

We certainly can't lay out the benefits without the costs for the unconverted, but perhaps even more so we must be careful about this within the church. *We must be talking about the costs of following Christ with one another.* What does the gospel cost you, unmarried Christian? What does the gospel cost you, Christian businessperson? What does the gospel cost you, faithful pastor? What about you, college student? What does the gospel cost you, widow or widower? What does it cost *you*, dear reader?

The costs and demands of the gospel are some of the most vulnerable stories we hold, because they are sensitive and they are difficult and we're not always sure we're getting it right. These are the stories where our doubt and wrestling reside.

I can tell you what the gospel has demanded of me. Even typing that sentence brings tears to my eyes. I live where I live, write what I write, parent the way I parent, and spend my money and my time the way I do because of the gospel. I've said goodbye to people and places I didn't want to say goodbye to, I've struggled with loneliness, I've overlooked offenses, I've had to place others before myself in ways that made me feel invisible—all for the sake of the gospel. The cost of following Christ has seemed unbearable at times, especially when my flesh rises up, bucking for a fight.

The truth is that there is beauty in self-sacrifice, in casting away. I look back at all my wrestling against the claims of the cross and I'm beyond grateful that the cross has won. I'm still here. I'm still walking forward. The benefits of submission to Christ are becoming more and more joy-filled to me. And I also see the goodness of God to work on me slowly, otherwise I'd be crushed.

It's in losing that we are then able to seek and find the beauty of God and this big-picture story he's writing.

Losing is not easy, however. Choosing to release who we once were and what we once held dear is difficult and grievous. The bright and shiny beautiful things of the world are alluringly tempting at times. Privilege, power, worldly authority, physical glory, instant pleasure—we can often, if we're honest, envy the wicked for what they possess. How could these things not satisfy our ultimate desires? We plot for how we might gain both the cross and the world, baptizing our desires so we won't have to sacrifice or submit. When we stand on the side of the world and look at the cross, it seems foolish and unnecessarily demanding. We fail to see that we're headed to a different death than death that gains; this is a death that pierces and taunts and keeps the carrot forever dangling out of reach. It's a slow death we don't see coming until we've been filled to the brim with regret and misery.

The apostle Paul knew both beauties. He first knew the world's best beauty. Before becoming a Christian, he sat in the seat of religious authority and intellectual esteem, wielding power and enjoying great honor. He had it all. Then he collided with Jesus. He saw the dazzling worth and grace of Christ and fell on his face in submission, wanting all he could get of a world-surpassing beauty. There was no question what held higher value, and Paul gave his life to seek it. Listen to his reasoning: "I count everything as loss because of the surpassing worth of knowing Christ Jesus my Lord. For his sake I have suffered the loss of all things and count them as rubbish, in order that I may gain Christ" (Phil. 3:8).

Paul made a choice, and we must make a similar one. We're all seeking beauty, but are we seeking the beauty of redemption? If so, we must first count the world's offered beauty as loss.

We must walk away and never go back. We must keep company with the redeemed.

Because what encourages me when I'm faced with the call of the cross in a newly exposed area of my life is when I look around at the beloved people in my church and see that the cross is just as relentless in their lives. They are living, breathing movie trailers displaying the future redemption story. My single friends who want to be married could be traipsing around the city dating and sleeping with anyone and everyone. They could be taking their future into their own hands rather than waiting on the Lord and entrusting themselves to him. My married friends who have experienced difficulties in their marriages could be taking their spouses to divorce court. My same-sex attracted friends could be succumbing to their desires. All these hold steady in truth and grace for the sake of the gospel, and their stories not only compel me to do the same but also solidify our bonds of unity and friendship and show me anew the surpassing worth of the gospel.

When we keep company with the redeemed, we hear stories of redemption. We discover how God has authored and is authoring resurrection from death, and these stories urge us forward, help us keep fighting, and teach us that the Hero and his victors win in the end. It is the church—the multicolored wisdom of God—that allows us to fully see the beauty of God and the redemption story he's writing.

Shared Stories

I recall vividly the day my husband, Kyle, came home and revealed to me his good friend's serial adultery. This friend had confessed it all to him, desperate to repent and change. We were young in ministry and marriage, and I was shocked at the words I heard coming out of Kyle's mouth. Shock turned to tears of grief, because this good friend and his wife were (and still are) dear to us. I had no idea what to do or how to respond to his wife, but we were in it now and we'd be in it for as long as it took to see them through. Over months and years, I watched these two confess and forgive, and I watched God use this confession and forgiveness to restore a marriage that had been utterly broken apart by sin. They became to me a picture of the gospel and the power it holds.

Death to resurrection life.

A few years ago, just before Christmas, my husband answered the phone and I could tell immediately from his coded words that something had gone terribly wrong for the caller. He hung up the phone and told me, with permission, that a friend of ours had confessed adultery to his wife. Another one. Another desperate situation. This man had grown tired of carrying the guilt and shame and wanted to align his life

155

with what he said he believed. He was willing to walk through the pain of repentance and confession to get the grace he so desperately wanted and needed, but he'd sent his wife into a tailspin in the process. Our sin never affects just us, does it?

My husband linked the two couples from these two stories and simply asked the first to minister to the second. One husband telling another how to move forward in repentance. One wife exhorting another that forgiveness and restoration are possible with God's help. One couple pointing another to the cross and the costly beauty that's only available by walking through the pain of going down to the dirt of the self-death called confession.

And I have watched it all, taking notes. I've learned that the gospel is powerfully real. I've seen the bitter becoming sweet, mourning turned to laughing, beauty rising from the ashes. I've seen how God takes our stories within the larger story he's writing and draws others to know him.

These stories have fortified my faith. They have spoken wisdom into my own life and given me great hope, because I have my own desperate situations. When I'm disheartened under God's discipline in my life, or when I'm not certain I'll see in my sons' lives what I pray for them, or when I'm deeply wounded by a broken relationship, I recall these stories and many, many others of how "the reverse occurred"[3]—how God has wrung the most wonderful beauty out of the most horrific and seemingly hopeless circumstances.

It's interesting to me that Scripture often tells us to encourage one another by speaking of the day of the Lord, when all things will be made beautiful. Our stories within the big story—trailers, if you will—are the ways we fulfill that biblical command. Even when our redemption stories feel "complete" or resolved, we must share them often, because they speak the realities of the gospel, of a sure and steadfast hope, and of a further and final completeness to come. What an encouragement to those who are waiting well, counting all things loss, and doing the beautiful work of faith.

We're in a new day, church. We can no longer think of church as something we do, as if it's a social club or somewhere we go to get a shot of "feel better." We must instead help create a culture within our churches of familial friendship. We must be actively pursuing deep relationships with others within our churches in which we bravely share how the gospel is laying claim to our lives. Of course, this requires vulnerability, and not vulnerability simply for its own sake but so that we can know and be known in a way that helps us endure in truth and grace. If we don't do this, everyone stands apart as individuals, either not realizing how the gospel lays claim to them or believing they're the only ones having to give something up and, therefore, counting the cost as too great.

Church, this is a call to pursue and value familial friendship. We cannot call, for example, same-sex attracted people to submit their desires to Christ, quite possibly abandoning a dream for marriage, without offering the safe haven and deep companionship of lifelong family. We cannot call for singles to submit their sexual desires and hopes for marriage and children to Christ without also offering ourselves as their family. Church, listen to the words of our Christ:

> Peter began to say to [Jesus], "See, we have left everything and followed you." Jesus said, "Truly, I say to you, there is no one who has left house or brothers or sisters or mother or father or children or lands, for my sake and for the gospel,

who will not receive a hundredfold *now in this time*, houses and brothers and sisters and mothers and children and lands, with persecutions, and in the age to come eternal life." (Mark 10:28–30, emphasis added)

The call of the gospel is to walk away and never come back. We cast away so we may seek and find God and so that we may keep company with the redeemed. We belong now to Jesus. But he says that those who leave everything behind will be enveloped into family—the church. He describes the benefits of the Christian family as far outweighing the costs of submitting ourselves to Christ.

This is our way forward in these times. This is how we hold both grace and truth together rather than simply condemning or, on the other hand, loving without truth attached. We share our stories—because we all have them—of how Christ has laid claim to us and how we're wrestling to submit to him. We continually call our friends to die to self and live to God. We allow our friends to do the same for us. And as we call each other to walk away from who we once were, never to return, we invite them into a church that looks like family more than anything else.

A Sure Ending

We have the Spirit of Christ within us and we have each other. In the redemption stories of others, we find that the gospel is real and active. In remembering our own, we find hope and fuel for endurance. However, we must not just seek experiences. We must be seekers who know wisdom is found in Christ and that the way we know Christ is through Scripture.

God's Word to us is the script for the story. Our stories of redemption can only be found within that larger story.

This script tells us that there will be trouble in this life. We can predict with accuracy how it's all going to end, but we can't predict the twists and turns we'll have to navigate to get there. This can be scary. The process of wringing beauty, of God writing our redemption stories, will most assuredly involve conviction and painful transformation. There will be more things we have to lose so we have hands to hold the beauty we will gain.

But take heart, dear one! Redemption beauty is rich and satisfying. It will keep the heart full and happy for a lifetime. This kind of beauty won't let you grow bored and it will combat depression, anxiety, and sin. Stop seeking that which you have lost. Look forward. Watch expectantly for how God is going to redeem now in this life and wait eagerly for how he will fully redeem later in the next one.

The movie will one day be over, the credits will roll, and we'll have found our greatest desires coming true. The Hero and his fellow victors *will* win in the end.

God Is a Joy Whisperer

He Shows Us Beauty
When We Still Ourselves to Listen

For everything there is a season, and a time for
every matter under heaven: *a time to keep silence,
and a time to speak.*

D INNER BOILS ON THE STOVE, my children play somewhere in the house, and the to-do list screams in my
mind, but rather than attend to any of these things, I lean
against the kitchen counter and scroll mindlessly through
my phone. I'm instantly off in distant lands, my attention
spread as far and wide as where my Facebook friends live.

Someone is there beside me, speaking, but it takes several
moments for the words to register.

My senses, as if they're a computer restarting, reconnect
with my present surroundings. My son, freshly eleven, is there

at my side, standing perfectly still, looking at me with his big blue eyes, smiling and waiting for his words to register. His whispering voice is there in the moment that's passed, and I rewind to hear and comprehend.

Did he say what I think he said?

"I love you, Mom."

My sons, though loving and sweet, rarely walk up to me on a mundane Thursday and proclaim their devotion.

I stare at him, phone cradled between thumbs, and he stares at me, smiling, and suddenly his words, in all their sincerity and meaning, explode in my heart like fireworks. Pulling him to me, I wrap him up tight and hold on, refusing to let go until he's assured how much his words mean and, perhaps more importantly, that I've actually been present enough to hear them. At this age, he fits just under my nose, and I breathe in the smell of his mop of light brown hair. I feel the touch of his arms wrapped around my waist. I think of the sight of his smile from a few moments prior, when he patiently waited for his words to connect, and I lean down to kiss him firmly on his cheek. While another child slams the front door and the pasta boils and the to-do list screams, somehow we stand in a perfectly silent kitchen. His whisper has momentarily muted frivolous things and awakened me to ordinary beauty, making my heart sing.

Although my phone lies forgotten on the counter, it waits and even beckons, ready and more than willing to muddle my thoughts and blind me to everyday beauty, again and again and again.

I think about this moment later and picture myself standing at the counter, absorbed by my phone, completely oblivious to love and beauty. How many times have my children stood beside me, trying to get my attention, while I'm looking at pictures on Facebook of someone whom I can't quite remember ever meeting?

And suddenly I wonder how many times it's been that God himself has whispered in my ear, calling me to quiet myself, inviting me into his Word so he might remind me of his love, or has simply asked me to reflect on his goodness and faithfulness so that he might fuel me forward. How many times have I been oblivious to his hands stretched out, offering me beauty in the sacred mundane, because I'm instead swirling in all the infinite distractions I've chosen for myself?

Busyness, it seems, mutes beauty.

In Stillness, Truth and Life

I love being busy.

In one sense I love it because I desire to be actively engaged in significant work that honors God and that also utilizes the gifts he's given me.

However, my love of busyness has a prideful, dark underbelly, evidenced by my excessive busyness that seeks self-honor. Excessive busyness is a form of performance for myself and others. If I perform well enough—meeting every need presented to me, matching every standard I've set for myself—I believe I can avoid disappointing others and prevent the pain of having done so.

Excessive busyness mutes the truth that I'm not God, permitting my trust of self rather than the scarier thought of trusting God and disappointing others. A life characterized by excessive busyness, driven by a need to please, is demanding, constantly pushing me toward self-trust and self-exaltation.

So what happens when I cannot be busy because of illness? What happens in my heart when I know I've disappointed someone? What occurs within me when I've not met my own standards? What do I do when I'm aware of my need to change but my previous attempts at change have failed?

A sense of restlessness grows within me, pushing me to take control of the situation, try harder, and figure out a solution. Christian busywork, I call it. Anything resembling a three-point checklist for success, a vow of greater or more careful exertion next time, a trust in self in order to produce change. Busyness makes me believe I can outrun my restlessness, calm it by doing something about it *now*.

I recognize the same restlessness rising within when I experience pain. Busyness is an easy way to numb pain because it gives me some sense of mastery over what ails me, or at least some sense of movement within a difficult circumstance that stubbornly refuses to budge from my life.

I've learned to recognize and name my restlessness. It is uneasiness in my spirit; it is my flesh crying out, shouting loudly for attention. It is my opposition to the Spirit of God, who comes in a whisper and says, *Be still and know that I am God*. Keep silence.

This is not Christian busywork that does not actually work in the heart; this is Christian grace, calling me to still myself before him and surrender the pain, the sin, and the uneasiness into capable hands. This is a whisper of promise, of hope, of future joy, and I want these things so badly. However, keeping silence and listening for the whisper of truth regarding who God is and how he wants me to trust him is much harder than attempting my own Christian busywork. My flesh wars against the Spirit.

Why do we hate silence so? Why does our flesh war against the whisper? Why are we so rarely still? Perhaps it's that we cannot bear to face the reality and the emotions of the pain in our lives. Perhaps we willfully live opposed to God and are attempting to outrun his whispered conviction. Perhaps, as in my case, we believe our performance makes us approved and prevents pain.

It seems we don't want to have to think.

We just want to speak. We want to tell God what to do. We want to shout our name until the world attributes us fame. We want others to listen to us so we might be esteemed. We want to pronounce judgment, however premature, on what God is doing with us, especially within our suffering. We clamor for someone to meet our needs. We join the chorus of our critical world, adding to the noise and the ugliness, not realizing how this critical world is infusing us with distaste for the very whisper that is calling us to joy.

We must fight against the noise in order to still ourselves and listen.

I get up before my kids, stumble down the stairs to the coffee maker, pour myself a full cup, and sit down on the worn right cushion of my couch to read my Bible. This has become a routine for me after years of inconsistency and, frankly, having little desire or motivation for God's Word. But when my husband and I moved across the country from "home" and planted a church in our living room, I became desperate for a soul-anchor, for life-refueling words, for the very character of God. I found myself nodding along with Peter when he said, "Lord, to whom shall we go? You have the words of eternal life" (John 6:68).

This is the whisper I hear when life gets hectic and my soul is drained, when demands are high and motivation is low, when I've misplaced joy somewhere and cannot find it among my creature comforts. The Holy Spirit draws me back to the Word for sustenance, because in its pages are the words of life. I need the gospel of Jesus every day because I forget, because the world is noisy and distracting and, by it, my flesh is easily drawn away from joy.

When I still myself, I find life. God, whispering through the words of Scripture, speaks to my loneliness: "I am with you always, to the end of the age" (Matt. 28:20). He speaks to my need: "His divine power has granted to us all things that pertain to life and godliness" (2 Pet. 1:3). He reminds me of what is most important: "For in Christ Jesus neither circumcision nor uncircumcision counts for anything, but only faith working through love" (Gal. 5:6). He reminds me that he loves me: "See what kind of love the Father has given to us, that we should be called children of God" (1 John 3:1). And he reminds me that he sees what I do in honor of him: "For God is not unjust so as to overlook your work and the love that you have shown for his name in serving the saints, as you still do" (Heb. 6:10).

With these words in me, I can endure.

Silence Shows Us the Gifts

The world speaks judgment on those who choose to wait rather than instantly gratify, on those who take the long view, on those who place their hope in Someone they can't see. The world eats bitter fruit and offers us a taste, and because we aren't still and listening, we take and eat and grow bitter too.

It seems busyness is not the only beauty-muter. Bitterness is too.

And then, for the vast majority of us, there is consistent distraction.

This life is imperfect and painful, and its imperfection and pain come for us all. Mostly, however, life is routine and mundane. Dull. Uneventful. As we grow older, the events are typically not as happy as the eventfulness of our youth. Also, our eyes have been opened wide to all that can happen and does happen in this world. How easy it is to grow weary and cynical, how tempting to entertain away the rest of our lives. Entertainment, with its canned laughter and mindlessness. Then we don't have to think about anything, especially our fears and uncertainties and regrets. We don't have to make any changes; we just keep trucking along, doing what we've always done, whether or not it's good or right or God's will or working. We don't have to consider our chronic lack of joy. As if we're paralyzed and helpless, we simply let the dullness dull us, life turn us lifeless, the pain not profit us, the banality make us blank inside. *What's the point, really?* That's what we say to ourselves, even as we slip on our dress shoes and head to the office once again.

We're in good company, because these thoughts echo King Solomon's, who questioned everything and tried it all too.

I said in my heart, "Come now, I will test you with pleasure; enjoy yourself." But behold, this also was vanity. I said of laughter, "It is mad," and of pleasure, "What use is it?" I searched with my heart how to cheer my body with wine— my heart still guiding me with wisdom—and how to lay hold on folly, till I might see what was good for the children of man to do under heaven during the few days of their life. (Eccles. 2:1–3)

After considering the point of life, he came to this conclusion:

I perceived that there is nothing better for [people] than to be joyful and to do good as long as they live; also that everyone should eat and drink and take pleasure in all his toil—this is God's gift to man. (3:12–13)

What stands out to me in these words is that God is handing out good gifts and these gifts are the basic, even mundane, things of life: food and drink and fulfilling work. We're told we must make it our goal to enjoy the simplest of things, like strawberries and coffee and teaching multiplication tables to second graders. In other words, the routine and the mundane that we rarely think much about. But they are gifts in reach of all people—the bread, the water, the work of our hands—and Solomon, who went around the block a time or two, says this is it. *This is where beauty is found. This is where joy is found.* And it's available to all who receive it from God with grateful hearts.

If you think about it, this makes sense. These very parts of life—food, water, creation, dominion—are remnants of the Garden that, although marred and groaning, recall a better time when man and woman walked with God, joy unhindered. To receive the simplest building blocks of life— relationships, nurture and nurturing, sustenance, opportunities for cultivation, sun and rain—is to walk with God as Adam and Eve did.

We don't quite believe this is enough. The rich, the social media mavens, the leisured, the pampered, the hustlers and bustlers—they don't seem to be complaining. From our broken-down lives, they provide our happiness goals, so we busy ourselves up, dress ourselves up, fill ourselves up, grasping and seeking and climbing up, up, up; more, more, more. We try this and try that, and when it's not immediately to our satisfaction or a step toward what we want out of life, we're on to something else. What beauty we'll find when we get there, wherever the elusive *there* is!

This kind of living is a head-down, always moving, rarely thinking kind of living. In effect, when we do this we put beauty blinders of busyness, distraction, and consumption on ourselves and then wonder why in the world we are so prone to despair and cynicism. We're walking among manmade concrete when our hearts are made for the small wonders of God's creation.

Our hearts are made for thankfulness.

Silence Helps Us Notice

Creation still speaks—of God and how he is and what he does and what delights him—and one of the things it speaks is that there is a time for stillness and silence.

In the cycles and seasons of creation, loud gusts of wind flow over prairies, storms make cauldrons of waves, and cicadas cry out in summer heat. The cycles and seasons teach us most created things have volumes that can turn high and low. The ocean's water, in the most far-flung sea, stills. The ocean's water, pushed and prodded by hurricane winds, churns. Rain, falling from storehouses in the clouds or frozen into dropping ice pellets, loud as it hits the roof, turns soft and mesmerizing when the water forms into tiny fluttering snowflakes.

It's the snow, especially, that hushes the earth as a librarian moving among the shelves calling for quiet.

When it's snowing outside, I stand at the kitchen window with my coffee mug and try to watch individual snowflakes fall. Prior to the snow's arrival, when the forecast's been calling for eight to ten inches, there've been trips to the store for bread and milk, salt poured on the driveway, cars moved and wipers raised, shovels and sleds gathered from the shed, emails received from schools regarding inclement weather plans. At the sight of the first snowflake, my boys run through the house, ecstatic, begging to put on their winter boots and head outside. When they go, I stand again at the window, still, waiting for the quiet to descend.

After a few inches have accumulated, I go outside and listen. In our community, inches of snow shut everything down and shut everyone up in their homes. I hear no cars, no trucks on the highway a mile away. I hear only the snowflakes calmly falling to their final resting places, and this is precisely what I've come outside for—to hear the sound of peace.

After all the bustle of store runs and firewood gathering and chatter with neighbors regarding the forecast—rest.

In God's world, there are times when he directs the ocean to roar and the thunder to clap, but the snow is God's message to us that there is a time for silence.

On snow days, all work and strivings cease. My senses are awakened from their dull slumber to wonder at the design of a snowflake or the crackle of a fire in the fireplace.

This is what happens when we are silent—we notice. Like covering our eyes makes our hearing suddenly more alert, our purposeful silence and stillness offers us the opportunity to recognize beauty all around us just when we've found it difficult to see.

When was the last time you savored a bite of food? Took a walk in the woods? Listened to a bird's call? Held a child's hand and thoughtfully traced the shape of his fingers? Smelled fresh-cut grass? Stood under falling rain without an umbrella? Looked someone you love in the eye and really noticed them?

Friend, life isn't all doom and gloom. Certainly, there is pain. Certainly, mundane tasks require our attention, and, in general, we navigate uneventful days. However, let us have eyes to see and ears to hear. The invisible hand not only paints the invisible artwork of soul redemption but very visible beauty as well.

Let us be people who still ourselves so that our senses come alive. We must think in order to be thankful. And we must be thankful in order to experience joy. The greatest tragedies of our age are our constant motion, our overscheduled lives, and our obsessive attachment to screens. We tend to believe we'll be robbed of happiness if we fail to match the world's pace step for step when in fact this pace robs us of the simplicity that displays beauty, which in turn leads to thanksgiving and, after thanksgiving, joy.

If busyness mutes beauty, what mutes busyness? Beauty, of course. Paying attention to the small gifts of everyday life helps us see and savor and, in turn, makes our distracted, numb hearts beat with thankfulness.

Thankfulness will lead to joy, because when we're still, God himself will whisper it into our hearts.

Silence Leads to Speech

God is not often to be found in excessive busyness. He's certainly not dwelling in our loud bitterness. He's never in consistent distraction. He's found by those who purposefully seek him, who get still and small before him and listen for the timely truths found in Scripture and in his creation. The wonderful truth is that when we seek God, we find him, and he turns our eyes to beauty, even the beauty he promises to birth in our pain as we trust him.

It is not enough to be silent and still. We must quiet ourselves for the express purpose of looking, undistracted, for the beauty all around. When we're head-down, moving at the speed of light, heart and mind filled with the cacophony of myriad voices, we find ourselves wondering what we're doing all this for and why—and does it even matter? When we're silent, we are able to rediscover God and who we are in his story and rest again in the truest of true facts that Jesus loves us and will one day make beautiful things out of the inconsolable. In constant movement, the persistent and urgent voices seem truer than his.

I myself find that when I'm in constant motion and the volume of life is on high, I'm prone toward deep discouragement. A fog settles in that hides God from my view, and I can't find beauty anywhere around me.

There was a time when my husband and I were especially discouraged about our work and ministry within our community. We'd been laboring for souls and for our children and for each other, and we were exhausted. Problems seemed to have sprouted up all around us, and problems are persistently loud. They demand every ounce of energy and overshadow any good that is happening and, frankly, problems were all we could see in every direction.

Kyle and I had the opportunity to leave town for a few days together, so we hopped a train to New York City and held hands in silence for an hour or two in the train car until the urgent call of our everyday lives finally faded to silence. And then, still holding hands, we began to talk, speaking of God in hushed tones, aware suddenly of how he was working in our midst and how he had been all along. Only in silence could we hear again.

We were on a train but it felt as if we were flying above life in a helicopter, able to see from horizon to horizon for the first time in months. We began to recount and name even the smallest beauties we could look back and see: how God was working in a loved one's life, how he'd provided for us in specific ways, how he'd helped us through a difficult season, how he was growing in us a deep dependence upon him, how he'd given us gift upon gift through the people in our lives.

The day prior, I'd spoken of my heaviness and distress and wondered if we'd ever see fruit from our work. In the everyday grind we'd been blind, but now we could see, and I felt the burden lifted off of me by God himself.

In our stillness and silence, God spoke, reminding me of truth from Scripture I'd read months previous. I'd studied the book of Ezra, which recounts the historical story of the Jewish remnant returning from exile in Persia to rebuild the temple in Jerusalem.

In the beginning of the book, the remnant returns with great excitement. The older men who'd seen the original temple before it was destroyed stood weeping among the rubble, some crying tears of grief but likely also tears of gratitude at God's faithfulness to restore the broken-down walls and broken-down hearts. With anticipation, strong faith, and worship lingering in the air, they went to work.

We all know what that's like. Starting something is glorious. Stepping out in faith. Being awestruck by God. Experiencing moments of forgiveness and restoration. Knowing with assurance a specific calling by God. These are the job-change, baby-born, move-in, start-a-business, take-on-a-task kind of days. These are exciting and glorious days, full of nervous excitement, when God feels near, we know how much we need him, and we see his gifts all around.

They are not ordinary days, in other words. The reality of gospel life in ordinary days is not romantic. Instead, the Christian life is day-in and day-out faithfulness that goes largely unseen and is sometimes unrewarded or unfruitful. It's easy to become blind to beauty and to forget where we are in God's story.

We're in the redemption phase, where rebuilding and restoration happen.

What happened with the temple builders in Jerusalem is what also happens in our lives: gospel work, no matter the kind, is always met with resistance. They immediately faced opposition. In fact, their enemies stood over them as they laid bricks, telling them to quit. Eventually, their enemies secured a stoppage order from the same Persian king who'd originally given the Jews permission to rebuild.

They stopped building. They wallowed in their discouragement, paralyzed by it for *fifteen years*. In those years, they went spiritually bankrupt, losing all joy and zeal for the work God had given them to do. I can just hear them saying what I so often say to myself in the noise and clutter of life:

What's the point anyway? Where is God in all of this? Why isn't he working? I don't have the heart for this anymore.

But someone was hunting for beauty in the stoppage; someone was listening in the silence. Someone was recounting what God had said he'd do and looking at the invisible big-picture story rather than the physical ruins and the spiritual chaos.

Two people, in fact: the prophets Haggai and Zechariah. They were sustained by the words and promises of God, filled with his Spirit, able to cut through the clamor to discern truth, and primed by their silence before him to then speak out.

Thankfully, we have their spoken words recorded in Scripture, words that God used to encourage Zerubbabel, the leader of the rebuilding effort, and the Jewish remnant to resume construction:

Yet now be strong, O Zerubbabel, declares the LORD. Be strong, O Joshua, son of Jehozadak, the high priest. Be strong, all you people of the land, declares the LORD. Work, for I am with you, declares the LORD of hosts, according to the covenant that I made with you when you came out of Egypt. My Spirit remains in your midst. Fear not. (Hag. 2:4–5)

Then he said to me, "This is the word of the LORD to Zerubbabel: Not by might, nor by power, but by my Spirit, says the LORD of hosts. Who are you, O great mountain? Before Zerubbabel you shall become a plain. And he shall bring forward the top stone amid shouts of 'Grace, grace to it!'"
Then the word of the LORD came to me, saying, "The hands of Zerubbabel have laid the foundation of this house; his hands shall also complete it. Then you will know that the LORD of hosts has sent me to you. For whoever has despised

the day of small things shall rejoice, and shall see the plumb line in the hand of Zerubbabel." (Zech. 4:6–10)

I thought about those words as we rode in silence on the train. In some ways, discouragement had spoken so loudly that I, too, had given up laboring in the work God had given me to do. Haggai seemed to stand beside me, speaking of God's presence with me, his promises to me, his Spirit within me. And then Zechariah chimed in, exhorting me not to despise the ordinary days or ordinary work. God can, in his grace, do a great and beautiful work, and he does it one day—even one brick—at a time.

Only in my silence was I able to hear the whisper again and only then could I speak to myself, to my husband, to those in my life waiting in desperation: God is beautiful and, therefore, the story he writes will reflect his beauty. His story will not end in ashes. It does begin with our self-made ashes—with rubble—but it only ever ends in beauty. Hold on for that beauty!

I'm speaking to you now, friend. Hold on for the beauty to come through your ashes!

Sometimes the hardest work is the waiting. When we're holding shattered dreams in our hands and nothing seems right, all we can see is the brokenness; all we can hear are the loud voices of shame, discouragement, and hopelessness. But when we still ourselves and still all the clamoring voices, when we return to the Scriptures and recall and remember that God is actually there, when we receive the everyday bread and the wine as blessed gifts, we find strength for our waiting-work. To silence ourselves is to do the work of wrestling our wandering hearts into trust once again, believing that one day all of this brokenness and suffering and backbreaking labor in the name of the Lord will be worth every tear and every drop of sweat.

Do not despise the day of small things. Do not despise the small beauties, for they are precisely where God is present and where he's working. Notice accessible beauty and it will feed your endurance for the beauty to come that is, as yet, out of reach.

In the stillness, in the silence, in the small gifts, even in the waiting-work, there is joy to be had in abundance.

Silence Leads to Singing

I once did a word study of *joy* everywhere it's found in the Bible, because I wondered if joy was something we choose or something God gives us. What I discovered is that it is both a choice and a gift. We are commanded to rejoice always, but the Holy Spirit also births a sense of joy in us when we live according to his help.

What surprised me the most was how closely tied joy is with seeing and remembering and how closely tied joy is with singing.

When we keep silence and take in God's creation:

Oh Lord my God,
When I in awesome wonder
Consider all the worlds
Thy hands have made,
I see the stars,
I hear the rolling thunder
Thy power throughout
The universe displayed.

When we keep silence and remember what God, in his
love, has done:

> And when I think of God,
> His son not sparing,
> Sent Him to die,
> I scarce can take it in;
> That on the cross, my burden
> gladly bearing He bled and died
> to take away my sin

When we keep silence and remind ourselves of the promises:

> When Christ shall come
> With shout of acclamation
> And take me home,
> What joy shall fill my heart!
> Then I shall bow
> With humble adoration,
> And then proclaim My God
> How great Thou art.

When we keep silence, our hearts are filled with thankfulness, and our lips are moved not just to speak of his works
but to sing:

> Then sings my soul,
> My Savior, God, to Thee;
> How great Thou art,
> How great Thou art!
> Then sings my soul,
> My Savior God, to Thee:

How great Thou art,
How great Thou art![1]

On the train, I thought about those prophets, speaking the construction back into motion. I thought about how often the New Testament writers tell us to encourage one another with the future coming of Christ. When we sit in silence, seeking the simple beauty to be had on this earth, letting God's words seep into our hearts, he turns our silence into speech—encouraging words, exhorting words, hopeful words to those around us who are doing the difficult work of faith, hope, and love.

The question must come: Are you consistently seeking space for silence and stillness before God? Are you finding consolation in the Word and courage to wait for the future King's return? Are you so filled up with this courage that it spills out onto others through exhortation?

When we go to the Well of Life rather than swimming in a stagnant pond of excessive busyness or consistent distraction, he seeps truth into our waiting hearts that makes us thankful and filled with joy. Where there is joy, there is a song on our lips, a word of encouragement to share, a prayer of deep trust. We not only need silence and stillness for ourselves, that we might see truth and beauty, but we need it for others who are walking a similarly hard road.

We must believe the whisper and let it make our hearts sing. Everything changes on the whisper.

God Is Our Pattern

We Display His Beauty When We Love Creatively

> For everything there is a season, and a time for
> every matter under heaven: *a time to love, and
> a time to hate.*

WITH MY SON'S CLASS, I go on a tour of Montpelier, the historic home of the fourth president of the United States, James Madison. We stand with our backs to his oversize yellow front door and gaze at a perfect view of the Blue Ridge Mountains before stepping inside the house with a tour guide. Together, we learn of Madison's role in framing the United States Constitution and we peek at the titles in his library that are said to have influenced his embrace of a democratic form of government. Finally, we file into a small rectangular bedroom, which turns out to have been Madison's personal retreat.

The tour guide points our attention toward the wallpaper, a shockingly bright pinkish-red design. The wallpaper is an exact re-creation based on the original, he says. They know what the original looked like because, when the house was being restored, workers found a mouse nest behind the walls of Madison's bedroom. Inside the nest were swatches of fabric, pieces of a letter written in Madison's handwriting, and scraps of the room's original wallpaper. "Apparently," the tour guide says, "mice are good preservationists." We all smile, delighted at generations of mice tucked behind a wall, keeping history alive.

We've literally stepped into an invisible, unseen age through the imitation and re-creation of a pattern, now displayed on the walls of Montpelier. Through a re-created pattern, now I know something about a specific point in time. I can imagine James Madison in his room, sitting at the desk writing a letter, turning to speak to his wife, Dolley, as she stands in the doorway. I can imagine the day he died, in this very room, with only a slave at his side. Living at the foot of these mountains myself, I can theorize why such bold colors were chosen for the walls—perhaps to brighten up the many overcast days that characterize this region.

It is through this re-created pattern that I'm aware of James Madison as a finite person, not merely a historic figure. I learn truth through the pattern, but I also experience a sense of mystery and wonder as a result of something as simple as wallpaper.

This seems to be the way of God as well. He hasn't left us alone without any evidence of who he is. As we've seen previously, his creation points to him, so clearly in fact that all people are said to be without any excuse of incomprehension. Creation follows a pattern almost as in parade: the moon in the sky makes way for the sun every day no matter where one stands on earth to see it. The pattern tells of his personhood—he is perfectly consistent—and he is available to all who trace the pattern back to him.

So we could be sure of him, God wove himself into the pattern of creation. He entered into it, becoming the pattern for some among us to touch and hear and dine with. We find him as our pattern in papyrus papers left behind and preserved for generations so that we might know him not only as a historic figure but as God himself and that we might step into a very real yet invisible, unseen world through a portal of beauty and truth.

We find, in Jesus, a pattern: we make a mess of things, God uses our mess to create the beauty of redemption, the beauty of redemption is meant to draw us to him so we might experience it personally, and the truth and beauty of redemption shoot out of us to point to him so that others may know him and be set free in him.

Jesus said he came to love and serve and set the captives free. These are not simply beautiful words but beautiful actions, and they must also be our pattern for living. To know him is to act like him in all the ways we're able.

Are we able to redeem? No.

Are we able to draw souls to Jesus? No, this role belongs to the Spirit of God.

But are we able to display our freedom as an invitation? Yes, absolutely.

To know him and to be like him is to be compellingly creative, not solely in the traditional sense of the word but rather the comprehensive: to use our unique roles, gifts, skills, opportunities, and relationships to compel others toward Christ. We can create wonder and even transformation with an apt word spoken. We can paint life on the canvas of hearts through generosity and service. We can do our vocational work excellently in the name of Jesus. Whether we'd describe ourselves as artists or not, we each can be compellingly creative if we live purposefully in the pattern of Jesus.

Creativity Can Be Worship

In order to be compellingly creative in the pattern of Jesus, we must first be free, because freedom is a cannon that shoots us out into the world.

For many years I was not a cannonball but rather a dutiful soldier lugging around a backpack of joyless obligation. What mattered were my self-governing rules, obligations, and tasks. I marched from one day to the next, eager to achieve something and, perhaps even more, eager to outpace my fears. My greatest fear was that I was secretly unloved. My endless litany of tasks might possibly secure me the love I so desperately wanted. My life added up to a list of rules and obligations, all formed under an umbrella of religion, meant to conquer the shame I felt and earn me secure love from God.

In those days, if I could've attributed a color to God's personality and character, it most assuredly would've been gray. Muted, boring, unattractive, disengaging, distant gray. I kept hearing he was light and bright, joy and love, which I imagined as yellow or orange or fiery red, yet peering through my lists and behaviors at him did not help me comprehend any color at all. He was like an old grainy black-and-white picture where the faces are perpetually blurred.

Someone deep inside, however, called out to me through my music lessons and creative writing assignments and school-assigned literature. If I'd paid more attention, I'd have noticed what I felt after memorizing Bach's "Jesu, Joy of Man's Desiring" for my piano recital or while reading Harper Lee's *To Kill a Mockingbird* or O. Henry's "The Gift of the Magi" for English class: wonder. I was transported into a sense of wonder, something far above my regimented world. I was made to think about things more profound than syllabi, makeup, or boys, things like injustice and sacrifice and mystery.

I didn't think about those things for long. Beauty was something that would have to wait. I had guilt to deal with. Fear to face. Checklists to get through in order to secure love for myself.

However, God, in his goodness, stored away those feelings in my memory, helping me later label my youthful experiences as moments of wonder. I didn't yet realize that beauty was a weapon against all of the monsters under my bed. I refused the greatest weapon and instead wielded my own poorly crafted cardboard sword. I thought life was meant to be molded and grasped by the achievers and performers, and through sheer work, a meaningful and happy existence might squeeze out.

The truth is much different, and suffering and failure humbled me into discovering it. What I found is all my ceaseless striving and proving gained me nothing. I'd only spun wheels, never moving even a millimeter closer to getting what I most wanted. When I finally acknowledged I was spiritually destitute, God came near and gave me everything. I realized we're all meant to be receivers and responders; we receive all our goodness and power and, filled with wonder, respond with worship.

The love I'd sought had been there, beckoning, all along.

The color of God burst like fireworks before me. Everywhere I looked in Scripture, I found the yellow and orange and fiery red I'd heard about—because I looked, finally, back at God through a lens of God's own securing love.

Finally I was free. Free from self-condemnation, free from proving myself, free from the uncertainty of my standing before God, and free from the weight of entangling sin.

My understanding of Jesus's gospel of grace had come into focus, and I was changed in a million different ways. At the core, I was transformed into an imitator. No longer an evaluated performer, a religious zealot moving through my rituals and rules, or a God-appeaser who attempted to move his hand by my actions, I was brought low before the King who'd made himself low for me. Knowing how God had moved toward me when I was an unworthy sinner, how could I not then, in imitation and in honor of him, move toward others? Through him, I found the ability to imitate him: to forgive, to serve, to sacrifice, and to enter into the difficulties of others.

I found out how to love.

True freedom doesn't lead us to exercise our freedom by returning to fleshly indulgence. This only twists grace into something unprofitable and loathsome and leads right back to the prison cell we were freed from. True freedom leads us to love and serve others as an act of wonder-filled worship of God.

I had not known how to do so before. Honestly, I hadn't much cared to, because above all I'd cared for myself and my standing before God and others. When the gospel came in to roost, the values of the paradox kingdom became my own: faith, hope, and love. And these intangible values played themselves out in the most tangible of ways. Although not drastically different than before, my actions and pursuits took on new meaning because they were, for the first time, fueled by the love of Christ.

For the Christian, compelling creativity is another term for worship.

Beauty created in imitation of the Beautiful.

Is Creativity Selfish?

Secondly, in order to be compellingly creative in the pattern of Jesus, we must think rightly of creativity.

Not surprisingly, in my gray-colored youth I believed creative pursuits were frivolous and unnecessary. When the gospel of grace seeped into my soul, however, the creative pursuits I'd believed were secondary or even a form of self-indulgence became a primary mode of worship and God-glory.

Just as the Montpelier restorers knew what Madison's original wallpaper looked like because of an ordinary family of mice, we are meant to display who the Creator is through our own creating. Through our work, we point to him, describe him, and adorn him. We're meant to be creative in imitation and honor of the One who is making all things beautiful. Christians, it seems, should be the most creative people, the ones who run straight into the mysteries and wonders of life, the ones who happily delight in beauty and use many mediums to point to the beauty of our King.

Why is it that we often are not? Why are we hesitant to pursue beauty-making as if it is not somehow productive? Why do we feel as if we need permission to be creative? Why do we tend to believe creativity is self-indulgent?

When I first began writing seriously, I wrestled with these questions. My children were young and my husband and I were planting a church, in our living room no less, and what purpose did it serve for me to give a few of my limited hours a week to writing words that would likely never be read? And yet I couldn't escape the raging compulsion within me to create. In its infancy, my desire to write and write well was a fragile dream, difficult even to admit to myself.

I struggled to give myself permission for what I most wanted to do, because I felt writing—unproductive creativity—was somehow selfish. I tried convincing myself that it was a made-up dream; how did I truly know God was in it? Who was I to think I could do this? What did I possibly have to say that might benefit another person? And the most pressing question: Why was I wasting perfectly good time that could go toward certainties like laundry or planning monthly menus for my family or volunteer work at the kids' school? Rather than a spiritual work, writing felt like self-indulgence, primarily because I wanted so desperately to do it.

I finally shared my secret desire with my husband, and apparently the secret was not a secret at all. Kyle simply turned to me and said, "I know. You talk about it through tears about every six months."

He told me to go for it, and I did. I began to spend two hours a week at Starbucks with a notebook (a notebook!) and a pen. For one hour and forty-five minutes I would wrestle with all the thoughts of selfishness and stupidity, and for fifteen minutes I would actually write embarrassingly bad prose. *And I loved it.* I didn't love the thought-wrestling, but I loved the actual writing and how it helped me clarify who God is and what he was doing in my life, and so I kept doing it.

Turns out, the wrestling *was* the benefit, at least in the beginning. The wrestling was like a drilling down into the core of me, where I discovered what had been trying to get out all along.

Worship.

Worship had been trying to get out. I read somewhere that when you do something that feels like worship, you've found your calling. Even from the very beginning, writing felt exactly like worship. Like I was made for it. Like I was hitting an invisible bull's-eye I'd not previously known existed. Like I was following a pattern. *Like my heart was singing.*

Persisting in a creative endeavor is not romantic, nor is it easy. However, a truth popped out at me as I continued in my wrestling: God himself had implanted this desire in me so that I might take something he himself had given me and turn it back to him as an offering.

Through this truth, the wrestling also refined my motivations. If creating is worship, it's only about God. It's about him, through him, and for him; it's not for me or about me. There actually were selfish desires attached to my writing pursuits, so in order for me to write as worship, I had to crucify my expectations for results. Those hopes only turned my worship inward and distorted whatever beauty I hoped to create. We don't create so everyone will look at us; we create so everyone will wonder at the Creator.

For beauty's sake, for God's sake, there is a time to hate. In order to imitate and honor God in our creating, we must hate self-indulgence and self-glory. We must not have an agenda in creativity aside from worship. We must wrestle within ourselves until we're able to cultivate beauty simply because we are loved and because we want to love and serve others. This is the pattern of Jesus.

We must not join in the world's pursuits of creativity for the sake of self. Certainly there is joy to be found in the simple acts of sketching, decorating, or playing an instrument. But the greatest joy is when we do it for God alone. This is why the apostle Paul could say, "Imitate me, just as I also imitate Christ" (1 Cor. 11:1). Because he wasn't so concerned that others saw *him* or followed *him*. He was hoping that they'd see something wondrous, something beautiful, in his life that would lead them back to their Creator. His eyes were on Jesus and he was asking others to put theirs on Jesus as well.

When I see beautiful art, when I hear beautiful music, when I see patterns and colors put together in fabrics, when I see pencil drawings or observe someone's ability to play the piano by ear, I am amazed—not at the person who created it but at the One who created the person.

Their creativity makes me worship.

Creativity Is Love

Creativity is not frivolous or secondary for the Christian. In fact, aside from social justice or intellectualism, in this time it may be one of the last remaining avenues we have for engaging the world in a way not only to which people are receptive but also that stokes their curiosity.

Creativity is a form of love, a bridge, a way of communicating that is nonthreatening.

Philip Yancey says,

> Perhaps the best way to convey the values we cherish is not to talk about them all the time, or to try and legislate them, but rather to create literature and art in which they fit as firmly embedded nails. . . . Even now the doctrinal creeds adopted by early councils of the church are repeated, in the works by Mozart and Haydn and Beethoven, by skilled professionals in every major city in the world. Hardened music critics are still susceptible to their power. Reviewing a recording of Brahms's *German Requiem*, Howell Circuit of the *San Francisco Chronicle* wrote, "The performance is divine (in several senses). It constitutes an overpowering experience, one which is not only technically and stylistically perfect, but moving in an uncanny/religious way. When the chorus sings of 'The living Christ,' even an atheist can believe in Him."[1]

This is a clarion call for us to pursue creativity that loves and serves others. We must push ourselves past the easy kitsch and see-through propaganda Christians are known by in the world to create in richer, more profound, more realistic, and more excellent ways. We can only do so when we allow ourselves to grow in creativity—by giving it time and attention. We also can only do this when we ourselves search for and recognize true beauty, which requires cultivating wonder in our own hearts—which also takes time and attention.

Perhaps it is our own lack of wonder—our own lack of hope—that mutes our voice in the world. Without a soul transformed by hope, we have nothing to offer others, and we don't have a heart overflowing with figurative or literal song.

Certainly, in my own life, my obsession with regimented, religious living mercilessly mocked any hidden desire I had to pursue beauty. It felt wrong, somehow, to exult in what was exult-able about life, as if God expected me to trudge through it all. But when grace flooded in, wonder came in too. The gospel of Christ was so strange to my flesh, so surprising in its extent and volume, that I could do nothing but fall back into it with glad reception. This is the wonder that has led me to create. I want to write words that cause others to wonder at this grace. I want to try describing grace this way and then that way and then another way altogether so that the Holy Spirit in me might convey to the downtrodden and spiritually dead that there is hope indeed!

Although my life was characterized for years by self-condemnation and self-flagellation, I didn't realize how much I needed this grace. I didn't want to look at the reality of my life nor the reality of this world. It took me so long to see, and when I finally did, I saw darkness all around for perhaps the first time. This is, in fact, not morbid but rather a key component to understanding the gospel and, as a result, creating as a Christian. Our Christian kitsch betrays our preference for turning blind eyes to the reality of sin, darkness, and hopelessness in this world. We throw verses around like Band-Aids. We wrap up suffering in neat little bows as if the thirty minutes in the sitcom are almost up. We require that our songs consist of overtly Christian words and major chords. We have no patience for mystery, for nuance, for poignancy.

We must not be afraid to look, really look, at the realities of life. We must not convey that the inconsolable things don't exist. We of all people should be able to do so, because we know the extent of grace, we know the power the Holy Spirit has to transform hearts, we know a hope that holds like an anchor. God runs toward the brokenhearted and the suffering, the prostitutes and the beggars, so we, too, must run toward others with a song on our lips and a story on our tongues. How can we communicate to others in a way that might change their perspective, offer them true hope, and cause them to join in the wonder?

Frederick Buechner says we must create in a way that addresses the full human experience. He speaks to the preacher, a creator who uses speech to paint a picture. The preacher at the pulpit

is called to be human, and that is calling enough for any man. If he does not make real to them the human experience of what it is to cry into the storm and receive no answer, to be sick at heart and find no healing, then he becomes the only one there who seems not to have had that experience because most surely under their bonnets and shawls and jackets, under their afros and ponytails, all the others there have had it whether they talk of it or not. As much as anything else, it is their experience of the absence of God that has brought them there in search of his presence, and if the preacher does not speak of that and to that, then he becomes the captain of a ship who is the only one aboard who either does not know that the waves are twenty feet high and the decks awash or will not face up to it so that anything else he tries to say by way of hope and comfort and empowering becomes suspect on the basis of that one crucial ignorance or disingenuousness or cowardice or reluctance to speak in love any truths but the ones that people love to hear.[2]

This is creativity for the sake of worshiping God and loving and serving our neighbor: acknowledging that inconsolable things exist.

If God is making all things beautiful, if beautiful is the end of all of this, wouldn't he want us to draw traces of beauty and joy back to him from all points of the human existence, wherever they are, in praise and imitation of him? I think so.

This type of beauty, which starts in the muck and the mire, draws the world to sit up and take notice, not of us but of our beautiful Creator.

All Creators Creating

I sit with a friend over breakfast, our table squeezed in among other pairs of diners. We reach across to one another and hold hands for a brief moment. She has tears in her eyes and I have tears in mine, both of us tired and both of us broken over the state of things. She tells me her heaviness and I tell her mine, and I realize we're asking the same question of one another: *Does the work we're doing matter at all?*

In our own ways, we're each seeking redemption and reconciliation, for ourselves and for others. In trying so fervently to dispense hope and then discovering our impotency to right all wrongs, we've lost the very thing we've tried to give. We ourselves are empty and vulnerable. We feel invisible and wonder why we should care anymore. Why should we care for the disenfranchised? Why should we continue to shoulder responsibility? Why should we go on loving those who have wounded us so deeply? Why produce and cultivate when we could sit back and merely consume?

I'm reminded that creative work done in imitation of God is always focused on redemption, for this is his pattern. It's also fraught with difficulty. When we step out in front of the crowd, willing to lead and communicate and counsel and carry burdens, sometimes we stand alone and, many times, our work will be done through tears.

Solomon, in his brief treatise on beauty and time, says there is nothing better than to use what we've been given to do good in this life.[3] How, I wonder, is it better to sacrifice for the thankless than to seek my own good?

Because the most beautiful beauty in this life is redemption, and redemption only comes through sacrifice. Jesus sacrificed so our redemptive story could be written; if we are to create beauty in this life, it will involve imitating the Savior's sacrifice.

We must be in the mix, embracing the hard work. In the paradox kingdom, the greatest is a servant and the one who chooses to be last will one day be exalted to first. Although these are valued roles in the kingdom, they are thankless, invisible roles in the world. Who cares for the servant? Who supports the last in line? Who remembers the one at the bottom?

Those who do good creatively, who seek redemption persistently, find solace and help in the arms of the Suffering Servant. Our God is a God who sees the invisible and remembers what they have done in his name. This is why it's better to sacrifice than to self-indulge—it draws us close to the heart of our Savior.

His heart helps me continue on when I wonder where he's writing redemption, for when I'm embraced by him, I can also wait on him. Secure in him, I can then acknowledge there are things he left inconsolable and work faithfully, knowing that change or healing or beauty may not come quickly. We may need to walk alongside a friend for many seasons, bearing with them and they with us, until beautiful fruit is borne. In order to do this, we must be willing to engage doubts, temporary setbacks, questions, tears, and all of our own struggles to believe and endure that spring up in the process.

Perhaps you're waiting for something to be made beautiful. What can you do in the meantime? Give yourself to creative good. Give your life to love and serve in the ways you've been gifted. Draw your own perspective back to the small beauties of everyday life. Engage with others at the redemption level. Love others enough that you seek beauty for them as well as yourself.

One of my favorite aspects of how God designed the church is that we each have different ways of seeking redemption for others. We get to be creative according to where God has placed us and what story he's given us and what gifts and skills he's implanted in us. We don't all have to do good in the same ways. In fact, we mustn't, because we need every stitch in the whole pattern in order to draw the eye to the whole Christ.

I've recently recognized God calling me to lay down roles and take up influence, to be creative in doing good. How can I creatively use my influence, however small it is, in my community? The answer: to work toward change in the very things my friend and I were talking about over breakfast. Loving mercy, hating injustices, loving people, hating what keeps us from community with one another.

God has given us work to do. He has placed us in homes, in families, in neighborhoods and workplaces. How are you cultivating beauty? Craft your sermon with diligence. Receive your customers with joy. Proctor your class with excellence. Teach your children with love. Order your home with care. Embrace your suffering with patience.

Our creative work is a love offering.

And we need all creators creating.

SPRING

I love the world as it is, because I love what it will be.

N. D. Wilson[1]

Forever Beauty

For everything there is a season, and a time for
every matter under heaven: *a time for war, and
a time for peace.*

I N THE CITY, spring is coming.

Winter has been long and bitterly cold, as it always is.
My skin is dry and pale, and the trees are gray and bare,
and everyone has been hibernating in their homes after dark
each day.

But spring is coming.

This past weekend, the weather turned unseasonably warm
for February, the sun shone bright against a blue sky, and
the unnatural temperature was all anyone could talk about
around town. My boys played outside all weekend, eager to
drink in the warmth. One skipped to the street, raised his

hands in the air, leaned his head back with eyes closed, and twirled in circles as if in deep joy and gratitude for the end of winter. Standing at the dining room window, watching, I smiled and felt my heart twirl in circles of its own.

This is what spring feels like, and every year I stand on the heater grate in my kitchen, staring out the window, eagerly anticipating that feeling. We play Hide and Seek, spring and I. Spring hides beneath winter, and I seek its signs each morning when the sun rises.

I've discovered that there's an order to spring's unveiling. The forsythia is the harbinger of a Virginia spring, followed closely by the daffodils and redbud trees, with their pink and white flowers festooning the city. And then almost overnight, an explosion of crape myrtles, tulips, flowering plums, and crabapple trees coming out of their hiding places. From late spring into early summer, dogwood and magnolia trees bloom, as well as the azalea bushes right in my own front yard.

The spring fireworks always begin, though, with the forsythia.

My neighbor has forsythia bushes planted around her mailbox, and when, on my walks, I see the tiny flowers budding, I then begin my leaf vigil, checking daily for leaf buds on the oaks and maples around our home. That forsythia is a bright yellow taste of what's to come: color and life and longer, warmer days.

The order of spring speaks to the greater order of time: there was a time when the earth was born and, because of the fall, a time for all to die. There was a time for weeping and waiting for a deliverer, and a time when he appeared, saying and working the unexpected. There was a time to kill, and, blessedly, a time to heal. And now, we wait for the forsythia. We search for signs that the present weeping and waiting is almost over.

Winter, though barren with inconsolable things, is not death but merely dormancy.

If we were to put our ear to the fallow ground, we would hear a heartbeat thumping, pulsing beneath every point in time. Our first parents heard it in the beginning, when the earth was a newborn. We've heard it through the woodpecker and the doe. We've heard its echo through the seed of eternity planted inside each of us. We've heard it in our deepest pain and our happiest moments. The heartbeat of God has been there all along, unchanged, ever in pursuit of each one of us.

We heard it when God's people were enslaved, when

the people of Israel groaned because of their slavery and cried out for help. Their cry for rescue from slavery came up to God. And God heard their groaning, and God remembered his covenant with Abraham, with Isaac, and with Jacob. God saw the people of Israel—and God knew. (Exod. 2:23–25)

There was his heartbeat: God heard. God remembered. God saw. God knew.

When Zechariah recognized that the Messiah was coming, he prophesied, "Blessed be the Lord God of Israel, for he has visited and redeemed his people" (Luke 1:68).

Again his heartbeat, like a drum: God came for us and God redeemed.

In all of time, God has been there, unchanged. He has always been a God who enters in, takes on our grief, and never leaves.

He wants us to hear, to remember, to see, and to know that his heart beats for us. He loves us enough to have come for us and redeemed us, and he loves us enough to come back for us. In the meantime, he is engaged in our inconsolable things, grieving alongside us as we wait for death to turn to life.

The forsythia is like a distant drumbeat, and the redbuds and tulips are the sound of the drumbeat drawing nearer. The colors of spring are upon us.

The Drumbeat of War

When I was in high school, I was in the marching band. I played the flute but I loved the drums, and I especially loved when the drum line played solos. Something about their staccato sound got my blood pumping.

One year during football playoffs, in order to rally the team and spark school spirit, our band director had us march through the halls of the school in the middle of the school day. No one played but the drums, and when we were enclosed in hallways or under overhangs, their sound was absolutely deafening. All across campus, I imagine students and teachers alike strained to hear, trying to comprehend what exactly was happening right then in the middle of an ordinary calculus or biology class. As we approached, it became clear to them, and every classroom ground to a halt as we went by, students cheering and clapping along.

We marched out to the courtyard in the middle of the school's grounds, faced out in all directions, and played our school fight song so loud that we rattled the windows. The drummers went crazy upon our last note, leaning back and throwing all their weight into beating their drums.

There is something about a snare drum especially that rallies the troops and demoralizes the enemy with fear, no matter if you're on a high school football team or literally going into battle.

God's heartbeat is our rallying cry. Like a drum, he leads us into battle, because this present time is a time for war. This winter of waiting makes war on us, our flesh fighting against the Spirit and the beauty he wants to bring in the coming spring. Our flesh is blind and hard of hearing, and it pulls us backward into hopelessness.

Just before dark a few months ago, I picked up a friend for a trip across the mountain. Her house, nestled in the woods, was draped in colored lights and a green wreath hung slightly askew. The trees all around were bare and it was cold outside; the sky was gray. It was Christmastime and we'd planned to go together to see our favorite teenage ballerinas dance the parts of the Sugar Plum Fairy and the Dewdrop to "The Waltz of the Flowers" in *The Nutcracker*. My friend wore her fancy blue skirt with shimmery sparkles sewn in, the one she saves for special occasions. We've shared many of those together over the years, as well as occasions of deep heartache. She is a dear friend and, sitting beside her in the car that night, I remember falling back into the peace of familiarity and secure spaces.

I also remember that we tried hard to celebrate but we had heavy burdens we shared instead. We parked next to the historic theater and sat in the dark of the car, and I wanted to cry, but instead we went in and found our seats.

The Nutcracker began, but I couldn't think of anything but our conversation. I tried to think of how I might fix the problems we'd presented to one another. I tried to work through all the pieces, because I often believe if I think about it enough, I will come to some settled conclusion in my heart.

That night is what the waiting-winter feels like—it's full of worry, trying to control and fix, full of grief and brokenness. We move from skirmish to skirmish, a war within and a war without, because things are stubbornly imperfect.

Life is war for the Christian. As Rosaria Butterfield has said,

> We now have twin desires raging. The supernatural power that comes with being born again means that where I once had a single desire—one that says if it feels good, it must be who I really am—I now have twin desires that war within me: "For the desires of the flesh are against the Spirit, and the desires of the Spirit are against the flesh, for these are opposed to each other, to keep you from doing the things you want to do" (Gal. 5:17). And this war doesn't end until Glory.[1]

And yet, in the daily battle in the midst of this war, I hear the snare drum urging me forward. I hear it, and I remember I have weapons I can use to take up and fight. I have the Holy Spirit himself, my advocate in the struggle. I have the promises. And I have beauty.

Beauty is the weapon that will help me come through the war, and beauty is at the end of all this fighting.

A King of Peace

When Jesus arrived in Jerusalem on a donkey, he came with the vulnerability of being killable, torturable, betrayable, and deniable. Rather than put up a fight, he went willingly to the cross and the grave. He was oppressed and afflicted, yet he opened not his mouth.[2] He personally fought for and won our peace with God.

When he said he'd come back for us, his betrothed, we must know that he won't come on a donkey. He'll come instead on a war horse. John, in the vision God gave him of what is in our future, tells us:

> Then I saw heaven opened, and behold, a white horse! The one sitting on it is called Faithful and True, and in righteousness he judges and makes war. His eyes are like a flame of fire, and on his head are many diadems, and he has a name written that no one knows but himself. He is clothed in a robe dipped in blood, and the name by which he is called is The Word of God. And the armies of heaven, arrayed in fine linen, white and pure, were following him on white horses. From his mouth comes a sharp sword with which to strike down the nations, and he will rule them with a rod of iron. He will tread the winepress of the fury of the wrath of God the Almighty. On his robe and on his thigh he has a name written, King of kings and Lord of lords. (Rev. 19:11–16)

That passage used to frighten me, until I realized that Jesus will come back on a war horse to fight *for* me rather than against me, because I am "in him" and therefore inseparable from him. He will not come back as vulnerable and killable but rather as an invincible King. All of us who are in Christ will be victors with him on the final battlefield. The full power of Jesus's justice and holiness will be directed away from us and toward those who have resisted him. His fury will turn against the oppressors and those who've dealt unjustly,[3] and those who are in him will share in the spoils of peace and righteousness forever.

Through a final war, Jesus will set in motion all that we presently crave and dream of in the middle of our waiting-winter: a kingdom called All Things Beautiful.

We know we want all things to be made right, but do we know this kingdom? Is this future kingdom so real to us that even the thought of it lifts our heads and our hopes in this dormant winter? Is it so real to us that the expectation of the presence of Jesus and his affirmation of our endurance ("Well done, good and faithful servant") fuels us forward through temptation and trial? We must know this unseen kingdom more than we know what we can presently see.

We start by listening for the heartbeat, because at the center of any kingdom is the king. The heart of All Things Beautiful is Jesus Christ the King. He is the Prince of Peace. However, in order to bring final peace, he will first go to war against sin, wickedness, and injustice, to put them away forever. And the One who has experienced the most injustice to his name—Jesus Christ himself—will receive the honor due him. All will finally see and acknowledge him rightly, and all will fall to their knees at the revealed and clear truth of who he is.

A Kingdom of Peace

After Christ the King banishes his enemies, he will renew and restore all things under the banner of peace. The setting of All Things Beautiful is not an esoteric ideal; it is a place called the new earth. Isaiah prophesied of this, saying, "For behold, I create new heavens and a new earth, and the former things shall not be remembered or come into mind" (Isa. 65:17).

The former things shall not be remembered.

The creation that groans will shake loose its chains, and the predator and prey will not be remembered. Sin will be a forgotten memory and its consequences gone forever—no more murder, no more prisons, no more greed, no more reviling, no more oppression, no more betrayal, no more destruction. The fight of faith will be finished; there will no longer be fear or pride or jealousy to blind us, isolate us, and separate us.

In other words, there will be no more inconsolable things. Instead, the reverse will occur: we will be consoled in all things. Every grief and sorrow will turn to joy. All death will come to life. All that we create will be for good. This is a kingdom, built in the new earth around the New Jerusalem, of pure, unadulterated color:

> Then I saw a new heaven and a new earth, for the first heaven and the first earth had passed away, and the sea was no more. And I saw the holy city, new Jerusalem, coming down out of heaven from God, prepared as a bride adorned for her husband. And I heard a loud voice from the throne saying, "Behold, the dwelling place of God is with man. He will dwell with them, and they will be his people, and God himself will be with them as their God. He will wipe away every tear from their eyes, and death shall be no more, neither shall there be mourning, nor crying, nor pain anymore, for the former things have passed away."
>
> And he who was seated on the throne said, "Behold, I am making all things new." (Rev. 21:1–5)

The fight of faith will be over. In its place will be everlasting peace.

Every time Jewish people greet each other with *Shalom* [meaning peace], they express the God-given cry of the heart to live in a world where there's no sin, suffering, or death. There was once such a world, enjoyed by only two people and some animals. But there will again be such a world, enjoyed by all its inhabitants, including everyone who knows Christ.[4]

There is a time for war, but there will be a time for peace.
Jesus will get justice, and so will we.
Jesus has conquered death, and so will we.
Jesus will reign, and so will we reign with him.
All of your own inconsolable things—your miscarriage, your disability, your losses, your disease, your burdens—will be consoled and their grip on you forgotten.

This will be the end of the drumbeat of time, because limited time will give way to eternity. The heartbeat of God, however, will go on infinitely and it will be like a drumbeat rattling the windows—he will be near, and he will be visible! We'll get to see the jasper and carnelian of his appearance, and we'll hear him singing and laughing and talking. We'll know intimately the One we already love and long for now but cannot see. And we'll relate with others without even a hint of sin to separate us.

At the marriage supper of the Lamb, there will also be wedding presents. "After you have suffered a little while, the God of all grace, who has called you to his eternal glory in Christ, will himself restore, confirm, strengthen, and establish you" (1 Pet. 5:10). Not only will he restore what we've lost for the sake of Christ but we will also receive eternal glory. God will reward us and honor us according to the faith by which we lived in the midst of the waiting-winter.[5]

210

This reward will be Christ himself, and it will all have come through the enabling of his grace.

He will call those who were last to come first.

He will lift the lowliest to become the greatest.

He will make the weak forever strong.

He will make us rich in spirit rather than poor.

He will exalt the humble.

He will cause those who have given to receive.

He will give abundant gain to those who lost all for his sake.

He will remember and honor the faithful and obedient.

And for those who had grown weary in winter, he will usher in forever spring, where the tree of life is in constant bloom.

Time will become immaterial, as will waiting and promises and hope. But some things will remain in the kingdom.

We will create:

> They shall build houses and inhabit them;
>   they shall plant vineyards and eat their fruit.
> They shall not build and another inhabit;
>   they shall not plant and another eat;
>   for like the days of a tree shall the days of my people
>   be,
>   and my chosen shall long enjoy the work of their
>   hands. (Isa. 65:21–22)

We will have the ear of God:

> Before they call I will answer;
>   while they are yet speaking I will hear. (v. 24)

And we will enjoy him and enjoy others:

After this I looked, and behold, a great multitude that no one could number, from every nation, from all tribes and peoples and languages, standing before the throne and before the Lamb, clothed in white robes, with palm branches in their hands, and crying out with a loud voice, "Salvation belongs to our God who sits on the throne, and to the Lamb!" (Rev. 7:9–10)

All these will remain, forever beautiful.

We will finally know in full the beauty our hearts crave.

In our demand for present perfection, we create unnecessary wars and we are our own victims in the battle. However, if we fight to embrace the inconsolable things, knowing God grieves with us, knowing they are temporary, we not only can look forward with hope to a future forever peace but we can have peace in the present as well.

Arm yourself for the present fight with future beauty.

That's how Joseph fought, and why he made his children promise to carry his bones with them—because he believed by faith God would give them the Promised Land.

That's how Abraham fought as well—with faith. "For he was looking forward to the city that has foundations, whose designer and builder is God" (Heb. 11:10).

And that's how, when my son sits beside me in the car and asks, "Mom, is life hard?" and my insides twist and turn—because I know the true and right answer is mostly *yes*—I can also tell him how to arm himself for the war ahead.

Fighting with faith is the only way through.

When John describes his vision of the coming kingdom to those in waiting-winter, he stops several times and says, "Here is a call for the endurance and faith of the saints."[6]

In order to endure, we must join those who went before us:

> [Those who] died in faith, not having received the things promised, but having seen them and greeted them from afar, and having acknowledged that they were strangers and exiles on the earth. For people who speak thus make it clear that they are seeking a homeland . . . they desire a better country, that is, a heavenly one. Therefore God is not ashamed to be called their God, for he has prepared for them a city. (Heb. 11:13–16)

Here, too, is my call, saints, for your endurance and faith. Now is a time to find Jesus, hope, cultivate faith, groan for redemption, wait, and carry light and color into dark. Now is the time to seek beauty and discover the riches of God.

Because there will also be a time when you will no longer be standing at the window, searching, feet on the heater grate, heart groaning under the weight of winter. You will be outside, with your face to the sky, arms raised to the Son. You will have sown all your tears and you will reap with shouts of joy. Your mouth will be filled with laughter, and your heartbeat will rise like a drumbeat to match your king's. Joining in the nations' song, you will sing in rhythm with his heartbeat: *The Lord has done great things for us, and we are glad.*

And you will dance in the light and life of spring.

ACKNOWLEDGMENTS

I REALIZED IN THE WRITING PROCESS that this book represents my understanding of what faith in action looks like for the Christian. I've come to this understanding through my own difficult circumstances and as God has used them to strip me of many of my self-oriented beliefs. I'm grateful to my Father God, who has given me hope for this life and a life to come. May my words show his beauty.

This book has come through tears and much begging prayer. Thank you to those who have encouraged me onward: Susan, Amy, Marylyn, Jo, and, most of all, my beloved husband. Kyle, you are my greatest help, my steadiest champion, and my favorite person. The precise words you use in preaching often compel my own thinking and writing process. Thank you for valuing words and giving me eyes to see ancient truths anew, and thank you for your help in crafting this book. I'm indebted to you for its drumbeat imagery.

Will, Reese, and Luke, you delight me to no end. I love each of you and want more than anything else in life for you to know and embrace the beauty of God.

Mom and Dad, thank you for asking about this book and helping me carve out an extended period for editing and rewriting.

I'm grateful to the Baker Books team for giving me the opportunity to write this book, believing in its message, and helping me craft it.

Finally, Andrew Wolgemuth, I'm thankful for your work on my behalf and your ever-helpful perspective.

NOTES

Chapter 2 Marred Beauty

1. See Romans 1:30.
2. See Romans 1:25.
3. Edith Schaeffer, *The Hidden Art of Homemaking* (Wheaton: Tyndale House, 1971), 27.
4. See Genesis 3:15.
5. See Colossians 1:16.

Chapter 3 Unexpected Beauty

1. See Ecclesiastes 3:11.
2. See Galatians 3:8.
3. See Matthew 5:17.
4. Zack Eswine, *Sensing Jesus: Life and Ministry as a Human Being* (Wheaton, IL: Crossway, 2012), 96–98.
5. See the parable of the sower in Matthew 13:1–23.
6. See John 10:10.

Chapter 4 Beauty We Want to Avoid

1. See Mark 1:15.
2. Dictionary.com, s.v. "paradox," accessed July 10, 2017.
3. Matt Capps, "Five Reasons Christians Neglect Beauty in Theology," *The Gospel Coalition*, July 26, 2016, https://www.thegospelcoalition.org /article/5-reasons-christians-neglect-beauty-in-theology.
4. St. Aurelius Augustine, *Discourses on the Psalms*, public domain.
5. See John 14:3.

Chapter 5 God Is a Potter

1. "Notes on Ecclesiastes 3:11," *The ESV Study Bible* (Wheaton, IL: Crossway, 2012).
2. Matthew Henry, "Ecclesiastes," *Matthew Henry Commentary on the Whole Bible (Complete)*, retrieved from https://www.biblegateway.com/passage/?search=Ecclesiastes+3&version=ESV.
3. Ibid.

Chapter 6 God Is a Composer

1. R. C. Sproul, *Who Is the Holy Spirit?* (Sanford, FL: Reformation Trust, 2012), 32.
2. See John 16:7.
3. Owen Strachan, *Jonathan Edwards on Beauty* (Chicago: Moody, 2010).
4. "Notes on Ecclesiastes: 3:12–13," *ESV Study Bible*.
5. These thoughts and phrases were taken from a sermon given by my friend Louis DeLaura. I'm indebted to him for this understanding of walking by the Spirit.
6. Frances R. Havergal, "Take My Life and Let It Be," (1874), public domain.

Chapter 7 God Is Our Betrothed

1. See John 13:36.
2. See John 13:36.
3. John Piper, "A Shepherd and a Lion," *The Gospel Coalition*, June 18, 2016, http://resources.thegospelcoalition.org/library/a-shepherd-and-a-lion.
4. See Genesis 8:20; Exodus 17:15; Leviticus 17:11; 2 Samuel 24:25; Ezra 3:2.
5. See Esther 6:1.
6. Matthew Henry, "Ecclesiastes."
7. Ibid.

Chapter 8 God Is Our Color

1. Dictionary.com, s.v. "purity," accessed July 10, 2017.
2. See Galatians 2:20; 2 Corinthians 5:14–15.
3. Sinclair Ferguson, *The Whole Christ* (Wheaton, IL: Crossway, 2016), 44–45, emphasis in original.
4. See 2 Peter 3:11.
5. See Hebrews 5:8.

6. Dan Shapley, "Why Do Leaves Change Color in the Fall?" *Good Housekeeping*, October 15, 2012, http://www.goodhousekeeping.com /home/a18922/why-do-leaves-change-color-0909/.
7. See Hebrews 12:2; 2:10.
8. See Psalm 1.

Chapter 9 God Is an Author

1. Donald Miller, *A Million Miles in a Thousand Years* (Nashville: Thomas Nelson, 2011), 50.
2. Rosaria Butterfield, "Love Your Neighbor Enough to Speak Truth," *The Gospel Coalition*, October 31, 2016, https://www.thegospelcoalition .org/article/love-your-neighbor-enough-to-speak-truth.
3. See Esther 9:1.

Chapter 10 God Is a Joy Whisperer

1. Carl Gustav Boberg, "How Great Thou Art," trans. Stuart K. Hine (1949), © 1953, 1955, 1981 by Manna Music, Inc.

Chapter 11 God Is Our Pattern

1. Philip Yancey, *Vanishing Grace* (Grand Rapids: Zondervan, 2014), 140–41.
2. Frederick Buechner, *Telling the Truth: The Gospel as Tragedy, Comedy, and Fairy Tale* (New York: HarperOne, 1977), 40–41.
3. See Ecclesiastes 3:12.

Part Four Spring

1. N. D. Wilson, *Notes from the Tilt-a-Whirl* (Nashville: Thomas Nelson, 2009), 16.

Chapter 12 Forever Beauty

1. Rosaria Butterfield, "Love Your Neighbor Enough to Speak Truth."
2. See Isaiah 53:7.
3. See Isaiah 11:1–10.
4. Randy Alcorn, *Heaven* (Carol Stream, IL: Tyndale, 2004), 143.
5. See 1 Corinthians 3:14.
6. See Revelation 13:10; 14:12.

Christine Hoover is a pastor's wife, mom, speaker, and the author of *Messy Beautiful Friendship*, *From Good to Grace*, and *The Church Planting Wife*. She has written for *The Gospel Coalition*, *Desiring God*, and *Christianity Today*. Blogging at www.GraceCoversMe.com, she enjoys helping women apply the gift of God's grace to their daily lives. She lives in Virginia.

Follow Author

CHRISTINE HOOVER

Blog: GraceCoversMe.com

facebook.com/GraceCoversMe

@ChristineHoover

@ChristineHoover98

Also Available from

CHRISTINE HOOVER

LIKE THIS
BOOK?
Consider sharing it with others!

- Share or mention the book on your social media platforms. Use the hashtag **#SearchingForSpring**.

- Write a book review on your blog or on a retailer site.

- Pick up a copy for friends, family, or anyone who you think would enjoy and be challenged by its message.

- Share this message on **TWITTER**:
  "I loved #SearchingForSpring by @ChristineHoover"

- Share this message on **FACEBOOK**:
  "I loved #SearchingForSpring by @GraceCoversMe"

- Share this message on **INSTAGRAM**:
  "I loved #SearchingForSpring by @ChristineHoover98"

- Recommend this book for your book club, workplace, class, or church.

- Follow Baker Books on social media and tell us what you like.

 Facebook.com/ReadBakerBooks

🐦 @ReadBakerBooks